Baby Stuff

Contents

Hi, we're Aranzi Aronzo.
This book teaches you
how to make things
you'll need for your baby.
Well, maybe your baby
won't really need them,
but they're things that
might be fun to have.
Pregnancy is a magical time
unlike any other.
Having a baby is hard work,
but there will also be
plenty of things that
warm your heart.
Each day is like a fun
adventure.
Make the things in this book
while thinking of your baby,
your relative's baby or
even your friend's baby.

White Rabbit
Carefree.
She loves to eat,
have fun, and sleep.
Not so good with
the handicrafts.
She's best friends
with Brown Bunny.

Before You Start

Brown Bunny
She's cool, smart,
and responsible.
She has a knack for
handicrafts.
She sort of talks li[ke]
an old lady, though.
She's best friends
with White Rabbit.

Hi, I'm Brown Bunny.

01

Hey! White Rabbit here.

02

You can make all kinds of cute things for your baby by reading this book.

03

Wow, it looks like fun! Let's make lots of cute things for baby!

04

Wait, we're still just kids so we can't make babies.

05

That's fine. We'll make presents to give to our friends' and relatives' babies.

06

Still, I don't know what tools and materials to use when making these things.

07

Everything you'll need is written on the "Materials" page so you'll be ok!

08

Frequently Used Materials and Tools

Scissors
To cut patterns, cloth, felt, and thread

Glue
To glue on eyes, noses, and mouths
You can use either cloth glue or wood glue

Chalk Pencils
Chalk pencils are used to outline your patterns
Use light pencils for dark fabrics and dark pencils for light fabrics so that they stand out
Chalk pencils are useful because you can erase them even if you mess up
A simple colored pencil will do if you don't have a chalk pencil

Chalk Paper
Used when transferring a pattern onto fabric
Use chalk paper of a different color than the fabric so it stands out

Ruler
Used to measure lengths when making patterns

Sewing Needle
Used when sewing by hand
No particular length or thickness required
Use what works best for you

Embroidery Needle
For French Knot or Straight stitches using 3 or 6 threads
It is thicker and has a larger eye than the sewing needle

If you have one

Sewing Machine
If you have a sewing machine at home and can use it, we recommend you do so
You'll be able to work quickly with nice results

If you have one

Overlock Machine
Fabric won't fray if you sew around the edges with an overlock machine

Fabric
You can use the fabrics and colors specified in the respective "Materials" sections, or you can use fabrics and colors of your own choice
No one will get angry with you
Use the fabric of your choice!

Regular Thread
Standard No. 60 machine thread
Used to sew cloth
You can use it to sew by hand or by machine
Choose colors close to the colors of the fabrics

Embroidery Thread

Used to make eyes, noses, and mouths for the appliqués
Also used for cross-stitching (though you can use regular thread for cross-stitching as well)

Awl
Handy for turning the corners of bags, pouches, and purses right side out

Bodkin
Used when adding an elastic band to pants or a drawstring to a pouch

I'll explain about frequently used materials and tools

09

Before You Start

Look, look! I got all the tools and materials I need!

10

White Rabbit! Don't wave around sharp, pointy objects like that! It's dangerous.

Please be careful! Don't try that at home

11

I know, I know, I won't do it again. What should we do next?

12

First we make patterns. Patterns are on the "Patterns" page. It's easy!

13

How To Make Patterns

① If you need to enlarge to get the ideal size:

Copy Machine

enlarge to the ratio specified on the "Patterns" page

You can enlarge or reduce to ratios not specified in this book
Appliqués are especially fun to make in various sizes

② If there's no need to enlarge because the pattern is already at 100%:

Mr. Elephant

create the pattern by placing a thin piece of paper on top of the book and tracing it with a pencil
You can also create a pattern by making a photocopy at 100%

③ If the pattern is a square or rectangle, as with pouches, duvets and the growth chart:

you can make the pattern by measuring with a ruler instead of copying or enlarging

Once you've enlarged, traced or measured the pattern, cut it out
Your pattern is done!

14

I made the pattern! What's next?

15

We trace the pattern onto the fabric, then we cut the fabric along the traced line.

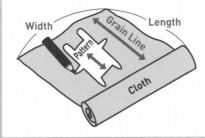

16

Tracing Pattern Onto Fabric

① Place pattern on fabric
② Trace using a chalk pencil
③ Cut fabric as traced

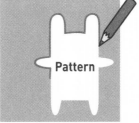

Pattern

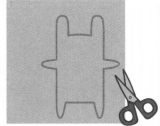

Width   Grain Line   Length
Pattern
Cloth

Jersey and stretchy terry cloth have a direction to the grain
The patterns have "grain line" written on them, too
Make sure the grain lines for the cloth and the pattern match up and trace the pattern using a chalk pencil

Elasticized fabric usually stretches more sideways than lengthwise

17

# Before You Start

18 By the way, what are zig-zag machines and overlock machines? What do they do?

19 Zig-zag machines and overlock machines are hardworking machines.

20 Fabric that frays easily can start to look like this along the edges after you cut it into patterns.
Zig-zag and Overlock machines keep that from happening.

Zig-zag Machine and Overlock Machine

How to "Keep fabric that frays easily from fraying"

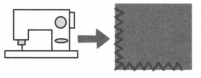

① Do a zig-zag stitch around the edges if your machine has a zig-zag function

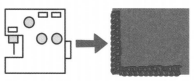

② Do an overlock stitch if you have an overlock machine

③ If you have neither a zig-zag function nor an overlock machine, apply sealant along the edges to prevent them from fraying

Fabric sealant is sold in crafts stores
If you seal the edges, the fabric will harden and won't easily fray
Read the instructions carefully when using the fabric sealant

22 If you don't care whether it frays or not, you can just sew the fabric together as is.

23 I don't care at all. I'll just leave it the way it is!

24 Hmm, I don't understand the part that says, "Sew along the dotted line."

25 When you see that, sew those parts with a machine or by hand. Either way is fine.

Sewing Along a Dotted Line

When Sewing by Machine | **When Sewing by Hand**

Do a straight stitch using the machine
It's good if you have a machine at home and can use it, because machines can sew faster and more neatly

1 Out
3 Out
2 In
Backstitch

Running stitch

26 Do a backstitch or running stitch when sewing by hand

27 1 strand, 6 strands, what's that about?

1 Strand, 2 Strands, 3 Strands, 6 Strands

 Birds of a feather thread together!

Threading 1 thread through your needle: "1 strand." Threading 6 strands through your needle: "6 strands"

1 thread: tie one end
2 threads: tie one end
1 thread: tie both ends together
3 threads: tie one end
6 threads: tie one end
3 threads: tie both ends together

1 Strand
Thread one thread through sewing needle

2 Strands
Thread 2 threads through embroidery needle
Or thread one thread through sewing needle and tie both ends

3 Strands
Thread 3 threads through embroidery needle

6 Strands
Thread 6 threads through embroidery needle
You can also thread 3 threads and tie both ends

28 When threading 1 strand use a sewing needle.
When threading 2 or more strands, use an embroidery needle.
The sewing needle eye is small so threading more than 1 strand through it is tough.

Before You Start

**Cross-stitch?
French Knot stitch?
I've never heard of those things!**
`29`

They're the names of different stitches. I'll explain in detail how to do them.
`30`

FK, S, B... It's like some code. I don't get it. This is impossible!
`31`

Those are just abbreviations. I'll explain.
`32`

Various Sewing and Stitching Techniques

Cross-stitch
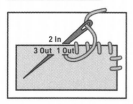
2 In
3 Out 1 Out

Overlock

View from side
View from top

You do an overlock stitch when you sew two pieces of fabric together

There are a lot of ways to stitch. The full names are written out so try to remember them!

B Stitch (Backstitch)

1 Out
3 Out 2 In

FN Stitch (French Knot stitch)

Turn twice — 1 Out
Turn 3 times — 1 Out
2 In

① When Making a Double French Knot, wrap thread around needle twice
When Making a Triple French Knot, wrap thread around needle three times

② With thread still wrapped around the needle, pierce fabric right next to where the thread comes out

③ Ta-da!
Often used for making eyes and noses

S-Stitch (Straight stitch)

2 In 1 Out
Bend slightly
Bend slightly

Makes a straight line Often used for making mouths

You can create smiling faces and other curvy lines by loosening an S-Stitch and applying glue to the back of the thread with a thin stick (a toothpick, for example)

Satin stitch
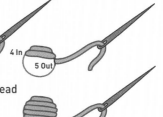 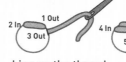
1 Out
2 In 3 Out 4 In 5 Out

Line up the thread parallel
Cover the area with thread
`33`

I have the materials and I kinda know what to do, but I don't know if I'll be able to make these things.
`34`

Don't worry too much about making it pretty or perfect.
`35`

The most important thing is to think of baby and make something that comes from the heart!
`36`

Yeah, that's it! Think about the new baby in the family and make lots and lots of heart-felt gifts!
`37`

Hello, Baby! We're Finger Puppets!
We can bend forward and backward.
We can even bow!
Don't be scared, let's be friends!

Finger Puppet Materials

Chalk pencils

Scissors

Glue
Glue

Embroidery needle
Used to sew FN and S-Stitches for eyes, noses, etc.

Sewing needle
Used for overlock stitches

Felt

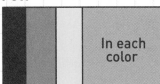
In each color

Embroidery thread
In each color

 # Finger Puppets Patterns and Instructions

How to Make a Raccoon Dog | Cut felt according to patterns

Ears, 2 pieces
Medium brown

White of eyes, 2 pieces
White

Patterns
Pattern at 100%

Eye area, 1 piece
Dark brown

Body, 2 pieces
Medium brown

Tummy, 1 piece
Peach

Mouth, 1 piece
Red

Glue on the tummy and eye area
Cross-stitch around the tummy

Glue on the white of eyes

Arms, 2 pieces
Medium brown

Insert ears and hands and overlock stitch around

Peach thread, 1 strand

Belly button: S-Stitch
Dark brown thread, 6 strands

Pupils: FN Stitch, turn 3 times
Dark brown thread, 6 strands

Glue on the mouth

Nose: FN Stitch, turn once
Dark brown thread, 6 strands

Medium brown thread, 1 strand

01

How to Make a Tiger | Cut felt according to patterns

Ears, 2 pieces
Yellow

Tummy, 1 piece
White

Patterns
Pattern at 100%

Nose, 1 piece
Black

Body, 2 pieces
Yellow

Mouth, 1 piece
Red

Arms, 2 pieces
Yellow

Glue on the tummy and cross-stitch around

Glue on the nose and mouth

Pupils: FN Stitch, turn 3 times
Black thread, 6 strands

Insert ears and hands and overlock stitch around

White thread, 1 strand

Whiskers and stripes: S-Stitch
Black thread, 6 strands

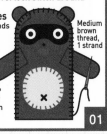

Yellow thread, 1 strand

02

09

Finger Puppets Patterns and Instructions

How to Make a Pig

Cut felt according to patterns

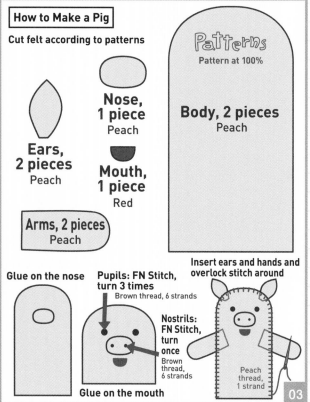

Patterns
Pattern at 100%

Ears, 2 pieces Peach

Nose, 1 piece Peach

Mouth, 1 piece Red

Arms, 2 pieces Peach

Body, 2 pieces Peach

Glue on the nose

Pupils: FN Stitch, turn 3 times
Brown thread, 6 strands

Nostrils: FN Stitch, turn once
Brown thread, 6 strands

Glue on the mouth

Insert ears and hands and overlock stitch around
Peach thread, 1 strand

03

How to Make a Penguin

Cut felt according to patterns

Patterns
Pattern at 100%

Stomach, 1 piece White

White of eyes, 2 pieces White

Arms, 2 pieces Black

Beak, 2 pieces Light yellow

Body, 2 pieces Black

Glue on the beak, eyes, and stomach
Cross-stitch around stomach
White thread, 1 strand

Pupils: FN Stitch, turn 3 times
Black thread, 6 strands

Insert ears and hands and overlock stitch around
Black thread, 1 strand

04

How to Make Terry

Cut felt according to patterns

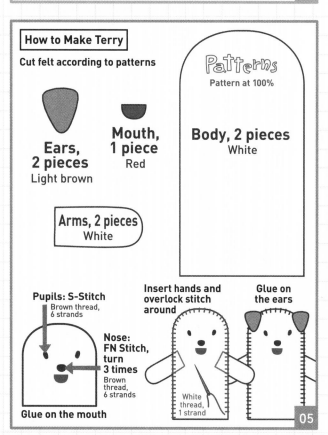

Patterns
Pattern at 100%

Ears, 2 pieces Light brown

Mouth, 1 piece Red

Arms, 2 pieces White

Body, 2 pieces White

Pupils: S-Stitch
Brown thread, 6 strands

Nose: FN Stitch, turn 3 times
Brown thread, 6 strands

Glue on the mouth

Insert hands and overlock stitch around
White thread, 1 strand

Glue on the ears

05

How to Make a Cat

Cut felt according to patterns

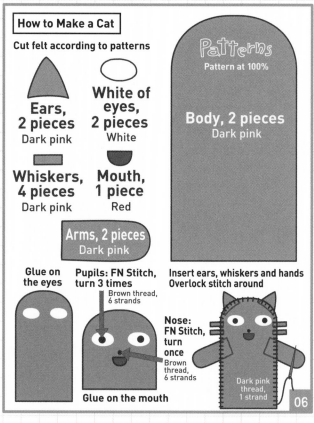

Patterns
Pattern at 100%

Ears, 2 pieces Dark pink

White of eyes, 2 pieces White

Whiskers, 4 pieces Dark pink

Mouth, 1 piece Red

Arms, 2 pieces Dark pink

Body, 2 pieces Dark pink

Glue on the eyes

Pupils: FN Stitch, turn 3 times
Brown thread, 6 strands

Nose: FN Stitch, turn once
Brown thread, 6 strands

Glue on the mouth

Insert ears, whiskers and hands
Overlock stitch around
Dark pink thread, 1 strand

06

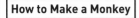 # Finger Puppets Patterns and Instructions

How to Make a Monkey

Cut felt according to patterns

Patterns
Pattern at 100%

Ears, 2 pieces
Orange

Face, 1 piece
Peach

Body, 2 pieces
Orange

Mouth, 1 piece
Red

Arms, 2 pieces
Orange

Glue on the face and cross-stitch around

Peach thread, 1 strand

Pupils: FN Stitch, turn 3 times
Brown thread, 6 strands

Under the nose to the mouth: S-Stitch
Brown thread, 6 strands

Nose: FN Stitch, turn once
Brown thread, 6 strands

Glue on the mouth

Insert ears and hands and overlock stitch around

Orange thread, 1 strand

07

How to Make a Bunny

Cut felt according to patterns

Patterns
Pattern at 100%

Ears, 2 pieces
Light pink

Mouth, 1 piece
Red

Body, 2 pieces
Light pink

Arms, 2 pieces
Light pink

Pupils: FN Stitch, turn 3 times
Brown thread, 6 strands

Nose: FN Stitch, turn once
Brown thread, 6 strands

Insert ears and hands and overlock stitch around

Light pink thread, 1 strand

Glue on the mouth

08

How to Make a Bear

Cut felt according to patterns

Patterns
Pattern at 100%

Ears, 2 pieces
Dark brown

White of eyes, 2 pieces
White

Body, 2 pieces
Dark brown

Mouth, 1 piece
Red

Muzzle, 1 piece
White

Arms, 2 pieces
Dark brown

Glue on the white of eyes and muzzle

Pupils: FN Stitch, turn 3 times
Brown thread, 6 strands

Nose: FN Stitch, turn once
Brown thread, 6 strands

Insert ears and hands and overlock stitch around

Dark brown thread, 1 strand

Glue on the mouth

09

How to Make a Panda

Cut felt according to patterns

Patterns
Pattern at 100%

Ears, 2 pieces
Black

Eyes, 2 pieces
Black

Body, 2 pieces
White

Mouth, 1 piece
Red

Arms, 2 pieces
Black

Glue on the eyes

Nose: FN Stitch, turn once
Black thread, 6 strands

Insert ears and hands and overlock stitch around

White thread, 1 strand

Glue on the mouth

10

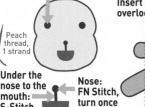 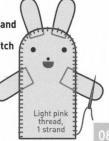

"If we're turned around like this, no one will recognize us, right?"
"Our faces are on our pants! They'll recognize us right away!"

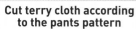 # How to Make Pants Rabbit and Pants Bear

01
Cut terry cloth according to the pants pattern

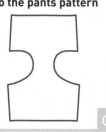

02
Using a zig-zag or overlock machine to sew the outer edge

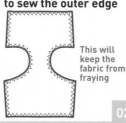

This will keep the fabric from fraying

03
Fold it in half inside out

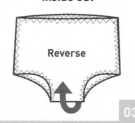

Reverse

04
Line up the sides and sew 1 cm from the outer edge

Reverse

White thread

05
Fold the top towards the reverse side about 2 cm then sew 1.5 cm from the top

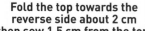

1.5 cm
White thread
Reverse

Leave 1.5 cm opening

Leave 1.5 cm open on the waist
You will thread elastic through there later

06
Fold up the edge of the leg opening about 1.8 cm

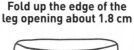

Reverse

07
Sew 1.3 cm from the outer edge

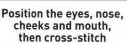

Leave open   Leave open
Reverse
1.3 cm

Leave a 1.5 cm opening on each leg
You will thread elastic through there later

08

Reverse

Turn right side out

Front

Backside of the front

The appliqué goes on the backside

If you can sew this much you can do the appliqué easily!

09
First is rabbit.

Cut terry cloth and felt according to patterns

Terry cloth

Felt

10
Stack the ears inside out and sew along the dotted red line

Turn right side out

Reverse   Reverse
White thread   Front
White thread

Fold in 1 cm from opening and sew shut

11
Position the eyes, nose, cheeks and mouth, then cross-stitch

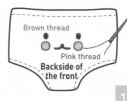

Brown thread
Pink thread
Backside of the front

12
Sew on the ears

Let the ears flop forward and stitch along the back of the ears

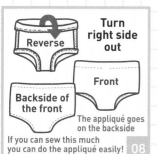

White thread

13
Now it is bear's turn

Cut terry cloth and felt according to patterns

Terry cloth

Felt

14
Stack the ears inside out and sew along the dotted white line

Turn right side out

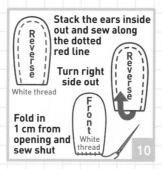

Reverse   Reverse
Brown thread
Front   Front
Brown thread

Fold in 1 cm from opening and sew shut

15
White thread

Stack the muzzles inside out and sew along the dotted red line

Turn right side out

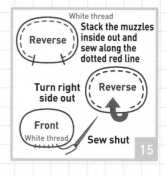

Reverse   Reverse
Front
White thread   **Sew shut**

16
Position the eyes, nose, mouth and muzzle, then cross-stitch

White thread   Brown thread
Backside of the front

17
Sew on the ears

Let the ears flop forward and stitch along the back of the ears

Brown thread

18
Insert elastic in the waistband and leg openings

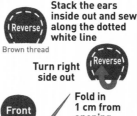 

Pull the elastic through the opening you left when you sewed the edges

19
Pull the elastic and tie at a comfortable size

Have baby try it on to get a good fit

Done!

Pants Rabbit and Pants Bear Materials

- **Chalk pencils**
- **Scissors**
- **Sewing needle**
- **Elastic** 5-8 mm wide flat-type
- **Bodkin** Used to thread drawstring through
- **Sewing machine**
- If you have one **Overlock machine**
- **Terry cloth** — White, Brown
- **Regular thread** — White, Brown
- **Felt** — White, Pink, Brown
- **Regular thread** (or embroidery thread) — White, Pink, Brown

Pants Rabbit and Pants Bear Pattern

Pattern is at 100%, so no need to enlarge

White of eyes, 2 pieces
White felt

Pupils, 2 pieces
Brown felt

Nose and Mouth, 1 piece
Brown felt

Ears, 4 pieces
Brown terry cloth

Ears, 4 pieces
White terry cloth

Muzzle, 2 pieces
White terry cloth

Opening

Cheeks, 2 pie[ces]
Pink felt

Eyes, 2 piece[s]
Brown felt

Nose and Mo[uth], 1 piece
Brown felt

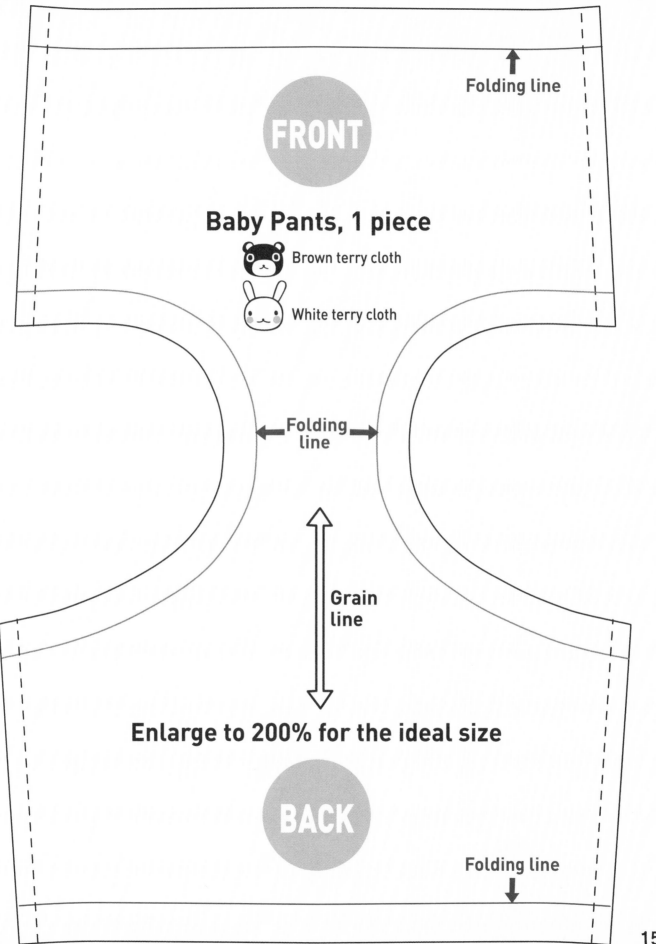

FRONT

Baby Pants, 1 piece

Brown terry cloth

White terry cloth

Folding line

Folding line

Grain line

Enlarge to 200% for the ideal size

BACK

Folding line

Little Spittle has drool running down but that doesn't mean he's a baby.
When Little Spittle sees something that looks yummy, he ends up drooling.
He should be called Little Glutton.

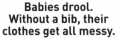

How to Make Little Spittle Bib

01
Babies drool. Without a bib, their clothes get all messy.

02
Fix the problem by putting a bib on baby.

03
But bibs get messy very quickly. Let's make lots of Little Spittle Bibs.

04
Because it's a spittle bib we named it Little Spittle. Let's make it!

Little Spittle

05
Cut fabric according to the patterns
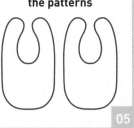

06
Prepare a piece of Velcro
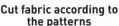
├─2.5 cm─┤
Any color
3 cm
Snip!
The corners are dangerous when they are pointy so round them off with a pair of scissors

07
Trace Little Spittle's face onto a piece of tracing paper

08
Decide where you want to position your embroidery
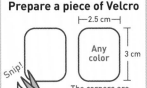
Around here?

09
Using chalk paper, trace Little Drool onto the fabric
Layer in this order from bottom to top
Fabric to embroider
Chalk paper (The pattern will be copied onto fabric as you trace over the chalk paper)
Tracing paper with pattern
Gently trace pattern for Little Spittle using a pencil

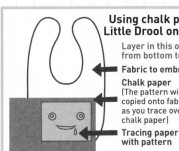
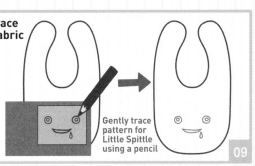

10
Backstitch over the traced lines (Embroidery thread, 6 strands)
Any color
After doing the pupils of the eyes in a Satin stitch, sew the outer part of the pupils using a B Stitch
It makes the pupils pop!
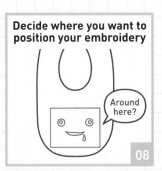

11
Stack the halves of bib inside out and sew along the dotted red line
Thread same color as fabric
Reverse

Cut along the blue lines
Reverse
Make incisions so the curve comes out neat and smooth
Be careful not to cut the thread!

Turn right side out
Reverse
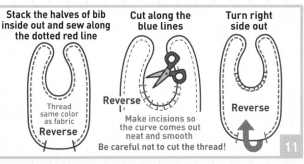

12
Put your hand inside and shape the bib
Front
Smooth out and then iron
Front
It will come out neater if you iron along the fold
Sew the opening shut
Front
Thread same color as fabric
Done!
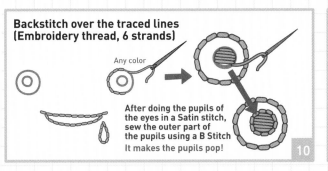
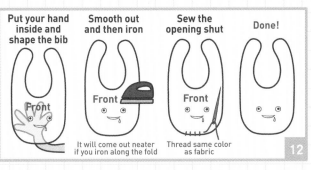

13
Sew around the edge of the Velcro
Be careful where you place the Velcro pieces
Front   Back
Done!
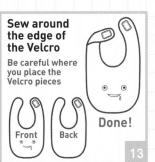

14
Now baby can drool away!

Little Spittle Bib Materials

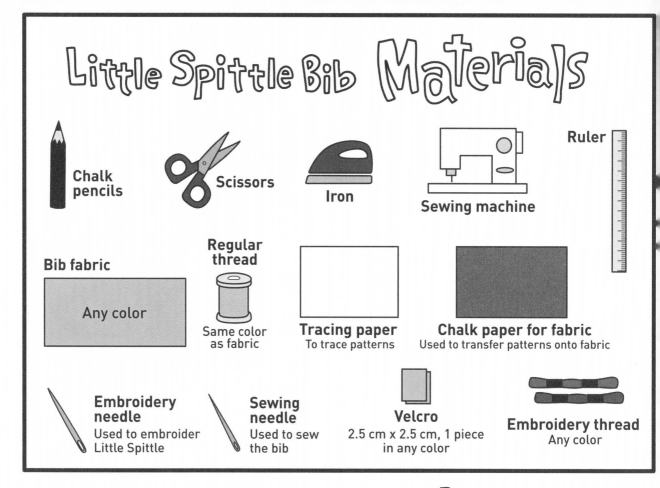

Chalk pencils

Scissors

Iron

Sewing machine

Ruler

Bib fabric
Any color

Regular thread
Same color as fabric

Tracing paper
To trace patterns

Chalk paper for fabric
Used to transfer patterns onto fabric

Embroidery needle
Used to embroider Little Spittle

Sewing needle
Used to sew the bib

Velcro
2.5 cm x 2.5 cm, 1 piece in any color

Embroidery thread
Any color

Little Spittle Bib Patterns

**Designs are at 100%,
but you can enlarge or reduce the size as you wish**

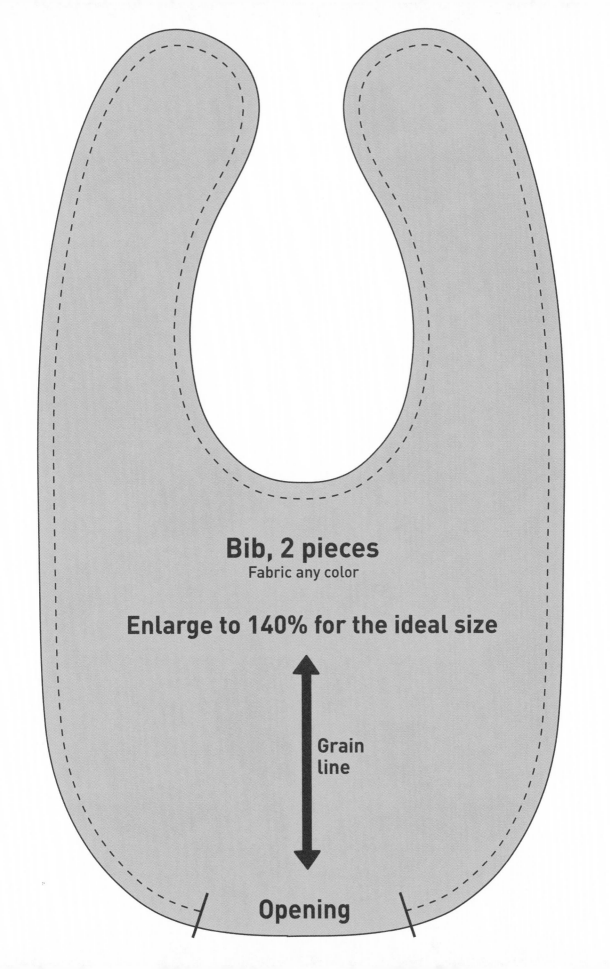

Bib, 2 pieces
Fabric any color

Enlarge to 140% for the ideal size

Grain
line

Opening

There's a yummy looking apple! Hello happy, fluffy Mr. Cloud!
Three bouncing bunnies, a puppy and oh! Yummy looking fish!
Meow! What a lively place!

How to Make Silhouette Appliqués

01
Let's try making simple and cute silhouette appliqués to put on baby's things!

Like a hat

or a vest

a bed guard

or a blanket

Cut the silhouette out of felt and add the mouth and eyes!

02
On light fabric use dark felt
On dark fabric use light felt
The silhouette will stand out
The colors can change depending on the silhouette

On red fabric, a white felt elephant

On blue, a brown elephant

03
Embroider the eyes, nose and mouth in any color you like

Dark blue eyes, red cheeks

Brown eyes, pink cheeks

04
One appliqué is fun! Combining several little appliqués is even more fun!

05
Cut felt according to the pattern

| Elephant |

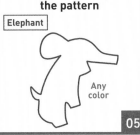

Any color

06
Position the appliqué then cross-stitch

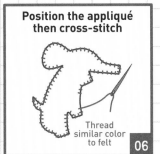

Thread similar color to felt

07
Cheeks: Satin stitch

Eyes: FN Stitch, turn once

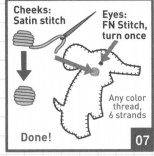

Any color thread, 6 strands

Done!

08
| Apple

Leaf: Satin stitch

Stem: B Stitch

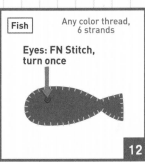

Any color thread, 6 strands

09
| Cloud

Any color thread, 6 strands

Eyes: FN Stitch, turn once

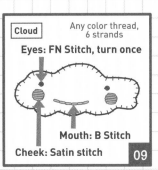

Mouth: B Stitch

Cheek: Satin stitch

10
| Bird

Eyes: FN Stitch, turn once

Eyes: FN Stitch, turn once

Any color thread, 6 strands

| Rabbit

11
| Snake

Any color thread, 6 strands

Eyes: FN Stitch, turn once

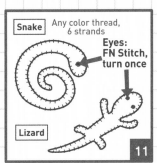

| Lizard

12
| Fish

Any color thread, 6 strands

Eyes: FN Stitch, turn once

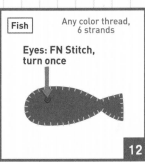

13
| Flower

Any color thread, 6 strands

Middle: FN Stitch, turn once

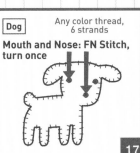

Stem: B Stitch

Leaf: Satin Stitch

14
| Butterfly

Any color thread, 6 strands

Eyes: FN Stitch, turn once

Antenna: B Stitch

15
| Horse

Any color thread, 6 strands

Eyes: FN Stitch, turn once

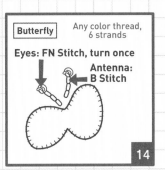

16
| Star

Eyes: FN Stitch, turn once

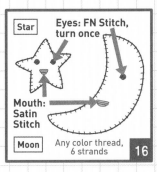

Mouth: Satin Stitch

| Moon

Any color thread, 6 strands

17
| Dog

Any color thread, 6 strands

Mouth and Nose: FN Stitch, turn once

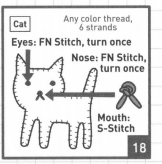

18
| Cat

Any color thread, 6 strands

Eyes: FN Stitch, turn once

Nose: FN Stitch, turn once

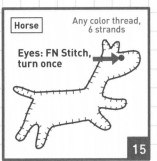

Mouth: S-Stitch

19
| Bear

Any color thread, 6 strands

Paws: FN Stitch, turn once

Eyes and Nose: FN Stitch, turn once

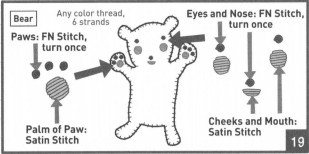

Palm of Paw: Satin Stitch

Cheeks and Mouth: Satin Stitch

Silhouette Appliqué  Materials

 Chalk pencils

 **Scissors**

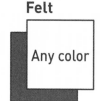 **Embroidery needle**
Used for FN Stitch, S-Stitch and B Stitch

 **Sewing needle**
Used for cross-stitch

Fabric for appliqués

Your choice of colors and materials

Felt

Any color

 Embroidery thread
Any color

Silhouette Appliqué Patterns

You can enlarge of reduce these patterns to exactly the size you want!

Bear

Butterfly

Bird

Flower

22

Star

Moon

Cloud

Horse

Dog

Cat

Apple

Lizard

Rabbit

Elephant

Snake

Fish

23

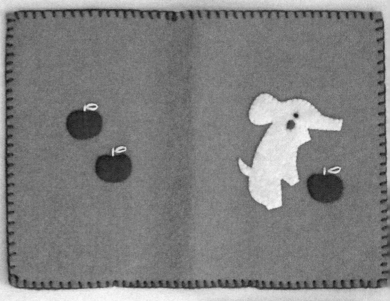

Mommy and Me

Handbook sizes aren't all the same.
Here are lots of different kinds of covers.
Anyone would be happy with any of the covers,
but some kids might say,
"I don't really like that picture!"

How to Make Handbook Covers

01
Let's make a handbook cover just for baby.

02
First off, let's start by practicing the BH stitch.

BH stitch (Button Hole Stitch)
It is named the "button hole stitch" because it is used to sew openings for buttons

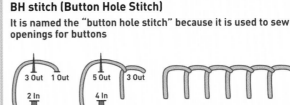

3 Out   1 Out
2 In

5 Out   3 Out
4 In

Repeat in the same order

03

04
Have you sharpened your BH stitch skills? Let's continue practicing

Prepare one small and one large piece of felt

05
Put the small piece on top of the large piece and sew around the small piece using the BH stitch

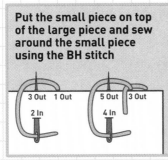

3 Out   1 Out
2 In

5 Out   3 Out
4 In

When you've sewn three sides, you've made a pocket!

06
Did you sew the pocket on well? We'll continue practicing

Take out two pieces of felt, each the same size

Lay one piece on top of the other, and stitch around using the BH stitch
Push the needle through the same spot on the back of the bottom piece of felt

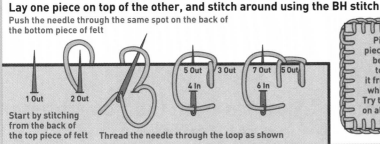

1 Out   2 Out

5 Out   3 Out
4 In

7 Out   5 Out
6 In

Start by stitching from the back of the top piece of felt

Thread the needle through the loop as shown

Pin the two pieces together beforehand to prevent it from slipping while you sew Try the BH stitch on all four sides

07

08
Did you sew the two pieces together well? Now you're a BH stitch pro. If you can do the BH stitch, making the notebook cover will be easy.

09
Measure the handbook you want to cover

Mommy and Me

B

A

10
Cut the felt

B − 3 cm

B + B + 1.5 cm

A + 1.5 cm

2 pieces A + 1.5 cm

10 cm
Card pocket 6.5 cm
If you want a card pocket

11
If you're putting on appliqués, add them at this stage

See the silhouette appliqués on page 20

12
Lay the pieces on top and BH stitch around the outside
Pin the two pieces together beforehand to prevent it from slipping while you sew

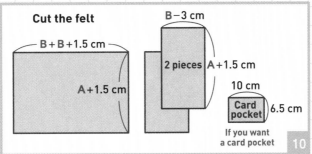

0.3 ~ 0.6 cm

0.3 ~ 0.5 cm

Approximate length of the BH stitch

Thread in any color. 3 to 6 strands (your choice)

If you want pockets on your note cover, sew the pockets on first

13
If you master the BH stitch, you can easily make any cover you want

Done!

If you make a big cover, you can have many pockets

You can make pockets like this

A pen holder is useful as well

You can make any pocket you like and place it wherever you want

25

Handbook Cover Materials

 Chalk pencils

Scissors

Embroidery needle
Use when sewing a BH Stitch, FN Stitch, S-Stitch and B stitch

Sewing needle
Use when sewing a cross-stitch

Felt for the cover

Any color

Felt for the appliqués

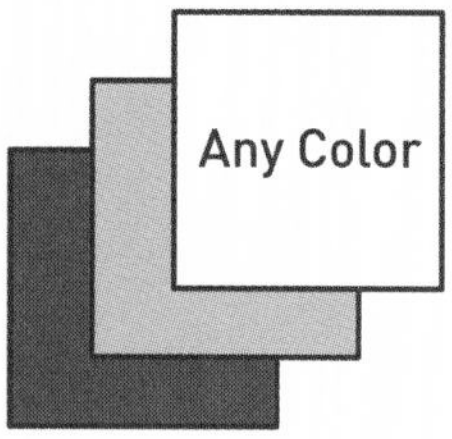

Any Color

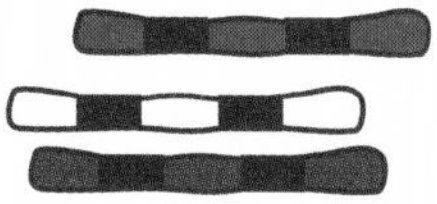

 **Embroidery thread**
Use for appliqués and when sewing a BH stitch
Any color

Handbook Cover Patterns

Measure your notebook and make a pattern from the measurement
Please use these as a reference
(Caution: your handbook's size may not be
any of the three given below)

It will be interesting to see what size handbook you have!

| Small | **Length 15 cm × Width 11 cm** |

| Medium | **Length 18 cm × Width 13 cm** |

| Large | **Length 21 cm × Width 15 cm** |

Mommy and Me

Pattern is at 100%, so no need to enlarge

Pen holder

Depending on the size of the pen, you can make this longer or shorter

Small pocket

You can make it larger or smaller, or change the shape!

For now, you can use these patterns as references. You can add other pockets in places you like as well!

Card holder

If you have larger cards, make this bigger!

These are my favorite bears!
I love them so much!
Make the same bear, you'll love it too!

How to Make My Favorite Bear

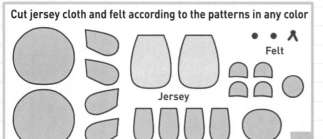

Cut jersey cloth and felt according to the patterns in any color

Felt

Jersey

01

Stack halves of the ears inside out and sew along the dotted red line

Reverse — Thread same color as jersey cloth

Reverse

Front — Cotton — Just a little cotton

Turn right side out and stuff with cotton

02

Stack halves of the arms inside out and sew along the dotted red line

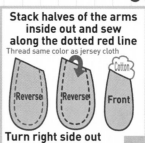

Thread same color as jersey cloth

Reverse Reverse Front Cotton

Turn right side out and stuff with cotton

03

Stack halves of the legs inside out and sew along the dotted red line

Thread same color as jersey cloth

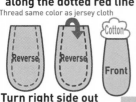

Reverse Reverse Front Cotton

Turn right side out and stuff with cotton

04

Sew along the dotted red line

Tail

Reverse Cotton — Thread same color as jersey cloth

Stuff cotton, pull the thread tight to turn it into a ball

Tight! Front

05

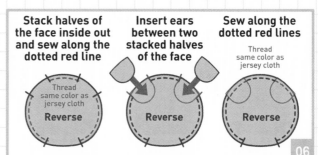

Stack halves of the face inside out and sew along the dotted red line

Thread same color as jersey cloth — Reverse

Insert ears between two stacked halves of the face

Reverse

Sew along the dotted red lines

Thread same color as jersey cloth — Reverse

06

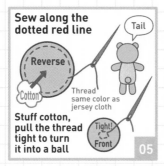

Turn right side out

Reverse

Stuff with cotton

Front — Cotton

Sew shut

Front — Thread same color as jersey cloth

07

Running stitch 0.3 cm from the edge of the muzzle

About 0.3 cm

Front — Thread same color as jersey cloth

When you fold back, it will easily form a clean curve

Pull the thread a little so it looks like this

Reverse

The edges of the reverse side will scrunch and bend, making it easier to fold under

Sew onto face with the edge folded toward the reverse side about 0.5 cm in

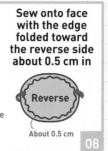

Reverse

About 0.5 cm

08

When sewing on the muzzle, it's cute if you stuff a little cotton inside

Thread same color as jersey cloth

Front — Cotton

Sewing the muzzle on with the reverse side scrunched up is a little hard, but you can do it. It's cute if it's a little bumpy

09

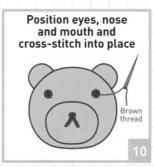

Position eyes, nose and mouth and cross-stitch into place

Brown thread

10

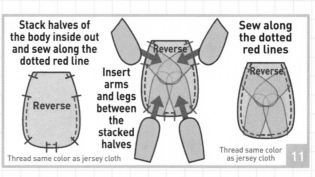

Stack halves of the body inside out and sew along the dotted red line

Reverse

Insert arms and legs between the stacked halves

Reverse

Sew along the dotted red lines

Reverse

Thread same color as jersey cloth

Thread same color as jersey cloth

11

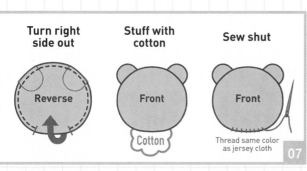

Turn right side out

Reverse

Stuff with cotton

Cotton — Front

Sew shut

Thread same color as jersey cloth — Front

12

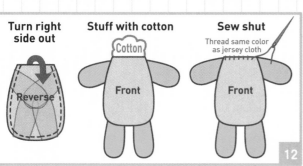

Sew the head onto the body

Make lots of bears in lots of colors!

Thread same color as face

13

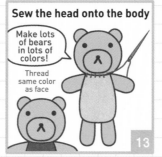

Sew on the tail

Sew it near my bum, please.

Done!

Thread same color as jersey cloth

14

My Favorite Bear Materials

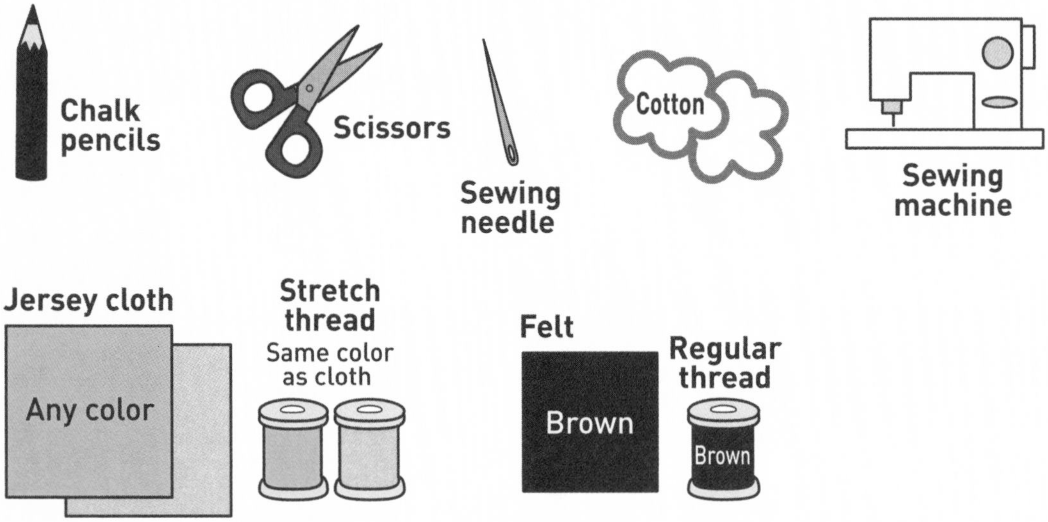

Chalk pencils

Scissors

Sewing needle

Cotton

Sewing machine

Jersey cloth
Any color

Stretch thread
Same color as cloth

Felt
Brown

Regular thread
Brown

My Favorite Bear Patterns

Pattern is at 100%, so no need to enlarge

 **Eyes, 2 pieces**
Brown felt

 Nose and Mouth, 1 piece
Brown felt

 **Ears, 4 pieces**
Jersey cloth any color

 **Muzzle, 1 piece**
Jersey cloth any color

 **Tail, 1 piece**
Jersey cloth any color

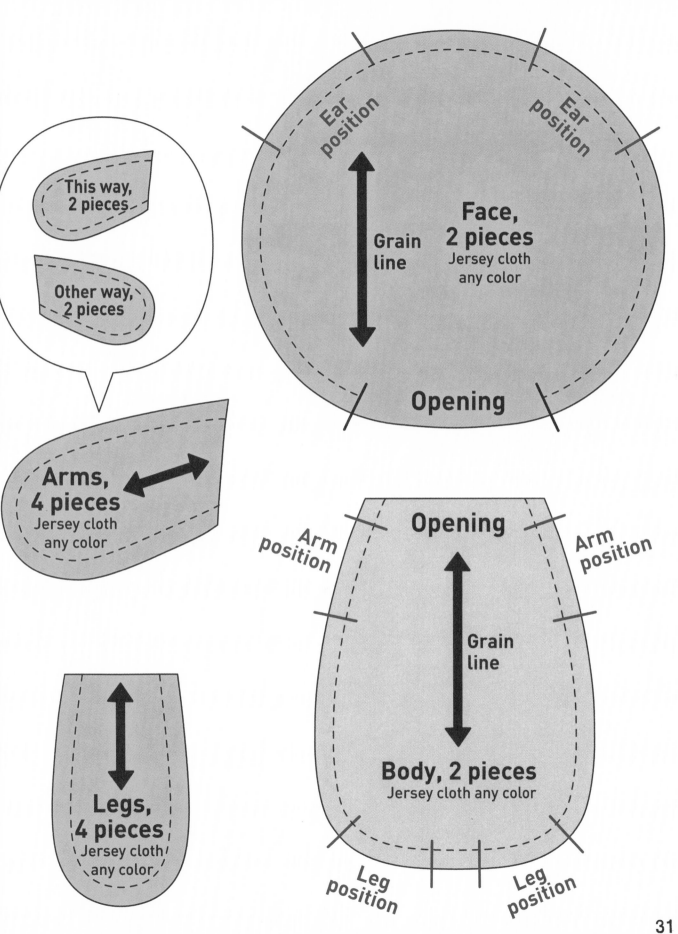

31

We are Flimsy Bunny
and Flopsy Bear.
We can flop around,
just like a towel.
We wipe away drool and sweat,
and even clean off hands!
Just leave it to us!

How to Make Towels

01

Babies are always drooling and sweating buckets
It's important to have lots of towels around every day

02

For some reason, babies love things that have tips and corners
Why is that?

03

Let's make a Towel for baby!
A towel that babies will really love!

Babies will probably love these parts

04

Cut the terry cloth according to the patterns

Thin terry cloth is best
Thick cloth is too stiff

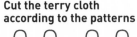

Bunny

Bear

05

Position the eyes, nose and mouth and draw with chalk pencil

Draw them in the place and size you like best

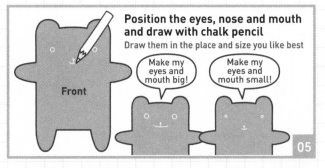

Front

Make my eyes and mouth big!

Make my eyes and mouth small!

06

Cut the eyes out of felt

07

Cross-stitch the eyes on

Brown thread

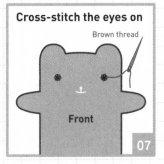

Front

08

Satin stitch the nose
(Embroidery thread, 6 strands)

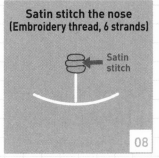

Satin stitch

09

B Stitch the mouth
(Embroidery thread, 6 strands)

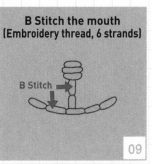

B Stitch

10

I have a face!

Front

11

Stack halves inside out and sew along the dotted red line

Reverse

Thread same color as terry cloth

12

Cut along the blue lines
Turn right side out

Make incisions so the fabric doesn't bunch
Be careful not to cut the thread

Reverse

13

Use the awl to turn out the tips of the arms and legs

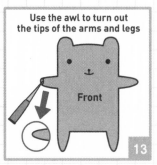

Front

14

Sew shut

Front

Thread same color as terry cloth

15

Done!

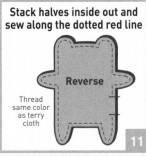

16

Make the bunny too!

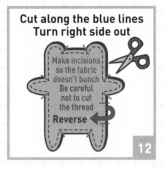

The bunny is made the same way

17

Bonus!

Cotton

If you put cotton inside, it can be a stuffed animal

Towels Materials

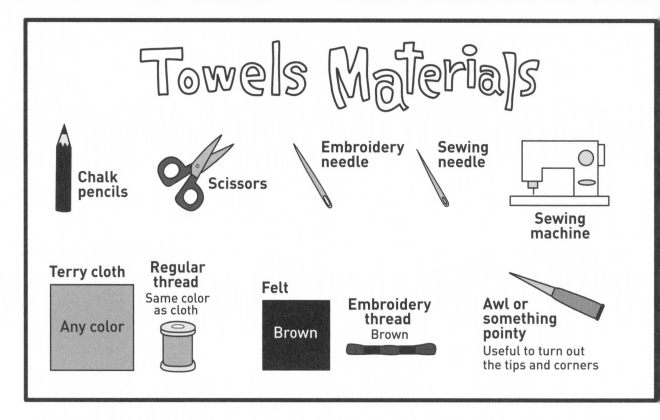

- Chalk pencils
- Scissors
- Embroidery needle
- Sewing needle
- Sewing machine
- Terry cloth — Any color
- Regular thread — Same color as cloth
- Felt — Brown
- Embroidery thread — Brown
- Awl or something pointy — Useful to turn out the tips and corners

Towels Patterns

**Patterns for the face are at 100% so no need to enlarge
But you do not have to follow the patterns
for the eyes, nose and mouth
You can do any size and any placement you like**

Eyes, 2 pieces
Brown felt

Nose
Satin stitch
Brown thread, 6 strands

Mouth
B Stitch
Brown thread, 6 strands

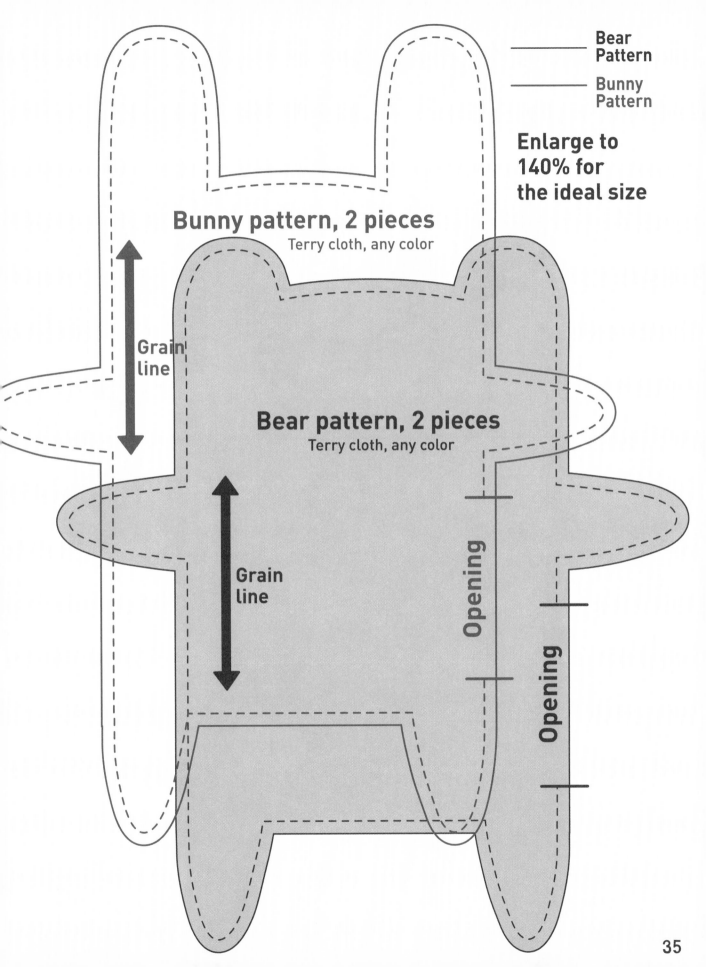

Bear Pattern

Bunny Pattern

Enlarge to 140% for the ideal size

Bunny pattern, 2 pieces
Terry cloth, any color

Grain line

Bear pattern, 2 pieces
Terry cloth, any color

Grain line

Opening

Opening

Opening

35

Little Bunny and Little Bear want to be baby's friend!
They want baby to squeeze them, teethe on them
and drool all over them!
Make baby some cute and fashionable little friends!

How to Make Lil' Friends

01 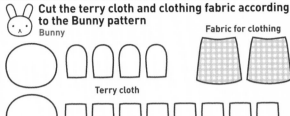 Cut the terry cloth and clothing fabric according to the Bunny pattern
Bunny
Fabric for clothing
Terry cloth

02  Cut the terry cloth and clothing fabric according to the Bear pattern
Bear
Felt
Fabric for clothing
Terry cloth

03 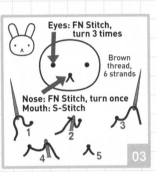 Eyes: FN Stitch, turn 3 times
Brown thread, 6 strands
Nose: FN Stitch, turn once
Mouth: S-Stitch
1 2 3 4 5

04  Glue the muzzle and white of the eyes on, and cross-stitch into place
White thread, 1 strand
Eyes: FN Stitch, turn 3 times
Nose: FN Stitch, turn once
Mouth: S-Stitch
Brown thread, 6 strands

05 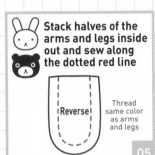 Stack halves of the arms and legs inside out and sew along the dotted red line
Reverse
Thread same color as arms and legs

06 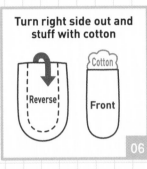 Turn right side out and stuff with cotton
Cotton
Reverse
Front

07 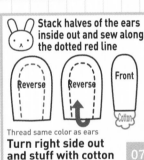 Stack halves of the ears inside out and sew along the dotted red line
Reverse Reverse Front
Cotton
Thread same color as ears
Turn right side out and stuff with cotton

08  Stack halves of the ears inside out and sew along the dotted white line
Thread same color as ears
Reverse Reverse Front
Turn right side out
Bear's ears are small, so you can't stuff them with cotton

09 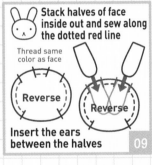 Stack halves of face inside out and sew along the dotted red line
Thread same color as face
Reverse Reverse
Insert the ears between the halves

10  Stack halves of face inside out and sew along the dotted white line
Thread same color as face
Reverse Reverse
Insert the ears between the halves

11  Sew along the dotted red line
Thread same color as face
Reverse Reverse

12  Turn right side out
Reverse Reverse

13  Stuff with cotton and sew shut
Thread same color as face
Cotton Cotton

14  Stack halves of the clothes inside out and sew along the dotted red line
Reverse
Thread similar to the clothing

15 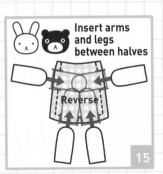 Insert arms and legs between halves
Reverse

16  Sew along the dotted red lines
Reverse
Reverse
Turn right side out

17  Stuff with cotton and sew shut
Cotton
Thread similar to the clothing
Front
Front

18  Sew the head onto the clothing
Thread same color as face
Done!

Lil' Friends Materials

Chalk pencils

Scissors

Glue

Sewing needle

Embroidery needle
Use for sewing on the eyes, nose and mouth

Sewing machine

Cotton

Embroidery thread
Brown for the eyes, nose and mouth

Stretch thread
Good for stretchy terry cloth

Terry cloth
Any color

Same color as terry cloth

Fabric for clothes
Any colors and any fabric

Regular thread
Close to the color of the clothing fabric

Felt
White

Regular thread
White

Height when complete (approximate)

Let's be friends!

Lil' Friends Patterns

Patterns at 100% so no need to enlarge

Bunny's patterns

Grain line

Ears, 4 pieces
Terry cloth, any color

Bear's patterns

Ears, 4 pieces
Terry cloth, any color

White of eyes, 2 pieces
White felt

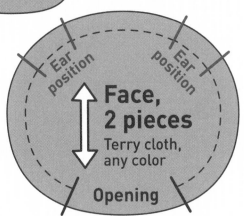

Muzzle, 1 piece
White felt

Ear position **Ear position**

Face, 2 pieces
Terry cloth, any color

Opening

Ear position **Ear position**

Face, 2 pieces
Terry cloth, any color

Opening

Opening

Arm position **Arm position**

Clothes, 2 pieces
Your choice of colors and patterns

Leg position **Leg position**

Opening

Arm position **Arm position**

Clothes, 2 pieces
Your choice of colors and patterns

Leg position **Leg position**

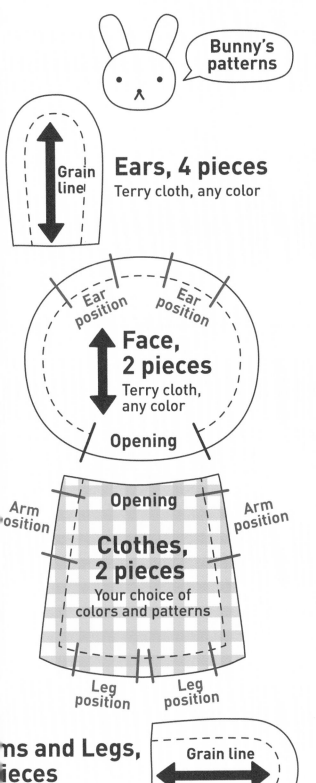

...ns and Legs, ...ieces
...cloth, any color

Grain line

Arms and Legs, 8 pieces
Terry cloth, any color

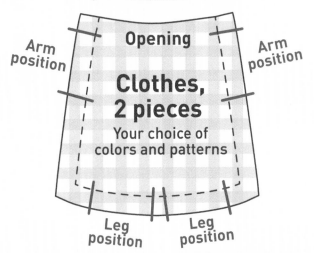
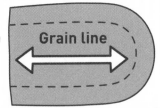

Grain line

I am Ms. Milk.
Put milk bottles in me.
I'll keep the baby's bottle nice and safe
because that's my job.

01
Ms. Milk is a bottle holder

Hello.

02
So Ms. Milk is good for holding bottles

That's right.

03
Cut the quilting fabric according to the patterns

Sleeve

Bottom

Quilting fabric frays easily so use a zig-zag or overlock machine around the edges to keep it from fraying

04
Fold in half inside out and sew along the dotted red line

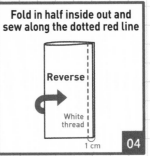

Reverse

White thread

1 cm

05
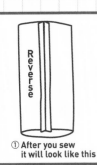

Reverse

① After you sew it will look like this

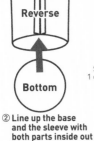

Reverse

Bottom

② Line up the base and the sleeve with both parts inside out

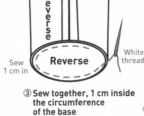

Reverse

Reverse

Sew 1 cm in

White thread

③ Sew together, 1 cm inside the circumference of the base
First do a simple running stitch

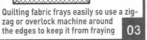

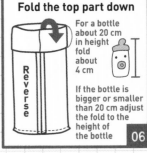

Reverse

Reverse

White thread

④ After doing a running stitch, sew with a machine or do a close hand stitch

06
Fold the top part down

Reverse

For a bottle about 20 cm in height fold about 4 cm

If the bottle is bigger or smaller than 20 cm adjust the fold to the height of the bottle

07
Cross-stitch

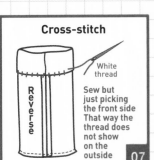

Reverse

White thread

Sew but just picking the front side That way the thread does not show on the outside

08
Turn right side out

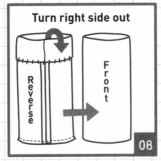

Reverse

Front

09
Cut the bottle nipple from any color of quilting fabric according to the pattern

10
Stack halves inside out and sew along the dotted white line

Reverse

Turn right side out and sew shut

Reverse

Front

Thread same color as fabric

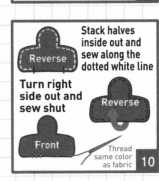

11
Lay the nipple over the top of the sleeve about 2 cm from the edge

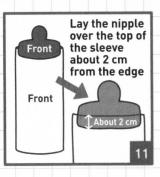

Front

Front

About 2 cm

12
Cross-stitch the nipple onto the bottle holder

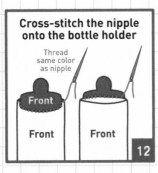

Thread same color as nipple

Front

Front

Front

13
Line up the two nipples on both sides evenly

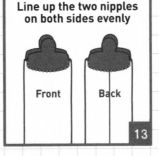

Front

Back

14
Cut Velcro according to pattern

Use Velcro close to the color of the fabric, or use white

Thread same color as Velcro

Front

Cross-stitch the Velcro onto the nipple

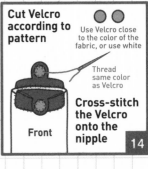

15
Cut the face according to the pattern

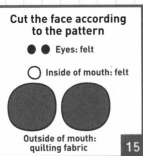

● ● Eyes: felt

○ Inside of mouth: felt

Outside of mouth: quilting fabric

16
Stack halves of the outside of the mouth inside out and sew along the dotted white line

Reverse

Turn right side out and sew shut

Reverse

Front

Thread same color as fabric

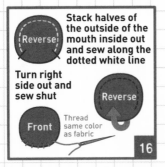

17
Position the eyes and mouth and cross-stitch into place

Brown thread

White thread

Thread same color as fabric

18
Make lots of Ms. Milk bottle holders for nursing fun.

Done!

Ms. Milk Bottle Holder Materials

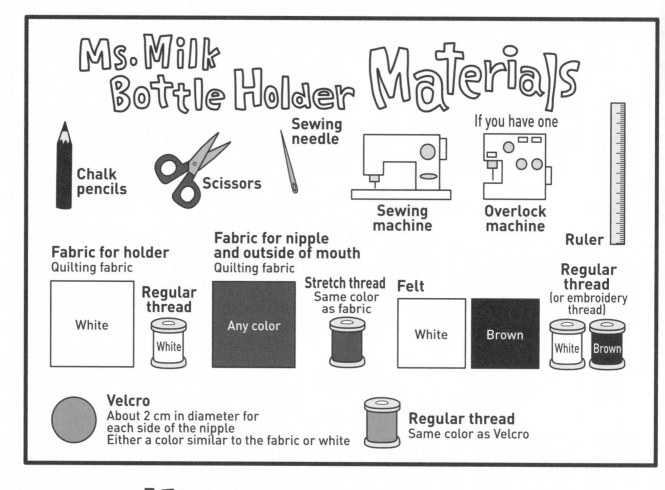

Chalk pencils

Scissors

Sewing needle

Sewing machine

If you have one
Overlock machine

Ruler

Fabric for holder
Quilting fabric
White

Regular thread
White

Fabric for nipple and outside of mouth
Quilting fabric
Any color

Stretch thread
Same color as fabric

Felt
White
Brown

Regular thread (or embroidery thread)
White
Brown

Velcro
About 2 cm in diameter for each side of the nipple
Either a color similar to the fabric or white

Regular thread
Same color as Velcro

Ms. Milk Bottle Holder Patterns

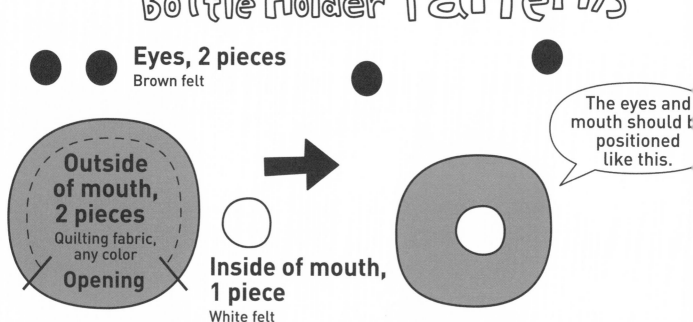

Eyes, 2 pieces
Brown felt

Outside of mouth, 2 pieces
Quilting fabric, any color
Opening

Inside of mouth, 1 piece
White felt

The eyes and mouth should be positioned like this.

Patterns of face at 100% so no need to enlarge

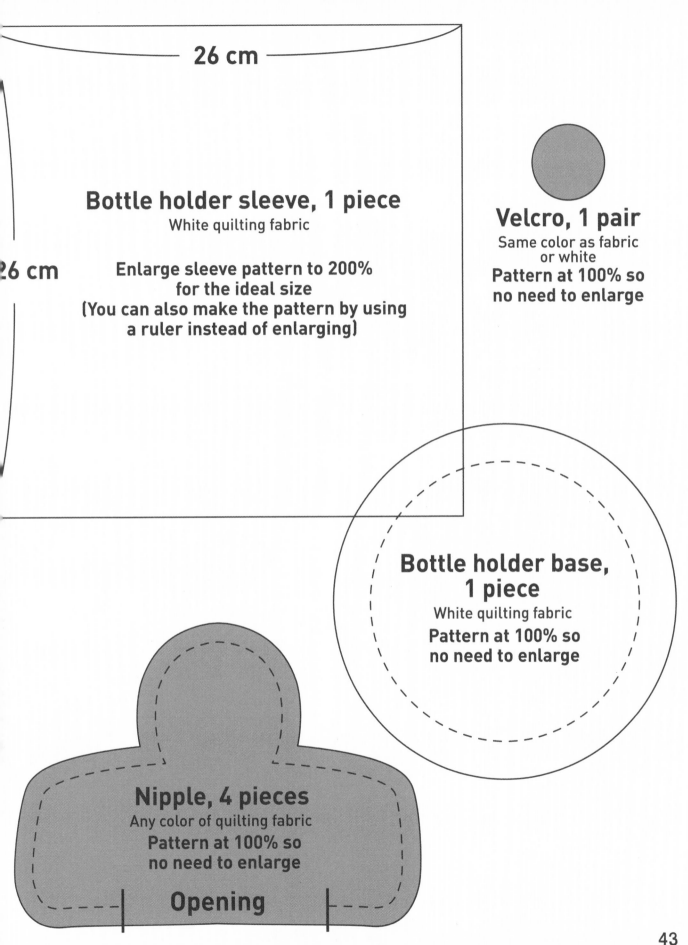

26 cm

Bottle holder sleeve, 1 piece
White quilting fabric

**Enlarge sleeve pattern to 200%
for the ideal size
(You can also make the pattern by using
a ruler instead of enlarging)**

26 cm

Velcro, 1 pair
Same color as fabric
or white
**Pattern at 100% so
no need to enlarge**

Bottle holder base,
1 piece
White quilting fabric
**Pattern at 100% so
no need to enlarge**

Nipple, 4 pieces
Any color of quilting fabric
**Pattern at 100% so
no need to enlarge**

Opening

43

Elephant, Bear, Rabbit,
Puppy and Kitty are all sleeping.
Baby would love falling asleep with this duvet.
Sweet dreams!

How to Make Bedtime Duvet

Measure the blanket

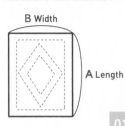

B Width
A Length

`01`

Decide on the final size of your duvet

B Width

If you want a snug fit, use the same size as the blanket

If you want it loose make it 1-3 cm bigger than the blanket

A Length

`02`

Cut the fabric for the Duvet

B + 4 cm

1
Cotton fabric
White

A + 2 cm

B + 2.5 cm

2 Cotton fabric White

20 cm

B + 2.5 cm

3
Cotton fabric
Checkered

A 16 cm

`03`

If you're worried about fraying, sew edges of the fabric with a zig-zag or overlock machine

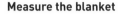

1 2 3

If fraying doesn't bother you, skip this step

`04`

Stack pieces 2 and 3 inside out and sew along the dotted red line

Line up the top edges

2 Reverse White thread 1 cm

3 Front

`05`

Fold the margin for a seam to 3 and iron

2 Reverse

3 Reverse

On the front sew along the dotted red line

White thread 0.3 cm

3 Front

`06`

Cut the fabric for appliqués according to patterns

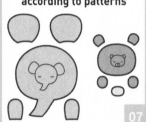

`07`

Cut the fabric for appliqués according to patterns

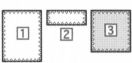

Use any color you want

`08`

Fold the edges of the appliqués back 0.5 cm

Fold
0.5 cm
Reverse
Fold

Reverse

It will come out neater if you iron it

`09`

With the edges still folded, place the appliqué and sew onto the duvet using a cross-stitch

Insert the ears just slightly into the head

Thread same color as fabric

Putting the face and hands over the edge of the blanket looks cute

`10`

Sew on the muzzle using a cross-stitch

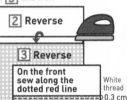

Thread same color as fabric

`11`

Nose: FN Stitch, turn 3 times

Below the Nose, Mouth: B Stitch

Brown thread, 6 strands

Brown thread

Eyes: B Stitch

`12`

With the edges still folded, place the appliqué and sew onto the duvet using a cross-stitch, thread same color as fabric

Eyes: B Stitch, Brown thread, 6 strands
Mouth: B Stitch, Brown thread, 6 strands
Dog's nose: FN Stitch, turn 3 times, Brown thread, 6 strands
Cat's whiskers: B Stitch, Thread same color as fabric, 6 strands

`13`

(Assembly)

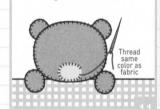

2 White thread

1 Reverse

3 Reverse

Sew about 1.3 cm in

White thread

Fold in about 1.5 cm and sew along the dotted red line

Fold 1.5 cm

`14`

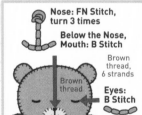

Line up 1.5 cm

Front   Front

1.5 cm

Front

`15`

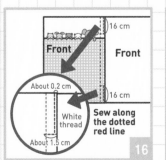

16 cm

Front   Front

About 0.2 cm

16 cm

White thread

Sew along the dotted red line

About 1.5 cm

`16`

Fold in half inside out and sew along the dotted red line

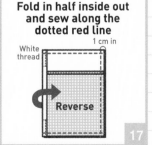

1 cm in

White thread

Reverse

`17`

Done!

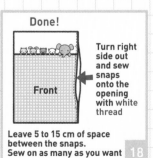

Turn right side out and sew snaps onto the opening with white thread

Front

Leave 5 to 15 cm of space between the snaps. Sew on as many as you want

`18`

Bedtime Duvet Materials

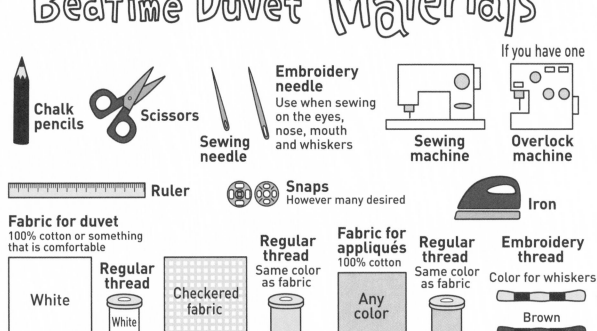

Chalk pencils

Scissors

Sewing needle

Embroidery needle
Use when sewing on the eyes, nose, mouth and whiskers

Sewing machine

If you have one

Overlock machine

Ruler

Snaps
However many desired

Iron

Fabric for duvet
100% cotton or something that is comfortable

White

Regular thread
White

Checkered fabric

Regular thread
Same color as fabric

Fabric for appliqués
100% cotton

Any color

Regular thread
Same color as fabric

Embroidery thread
Color for whiskers

Brown

Bedtime Duvet Appliqué Patterns

——————— **Cutting line**

– – – – – – – **Folding line**
(size of the finished appliqué)

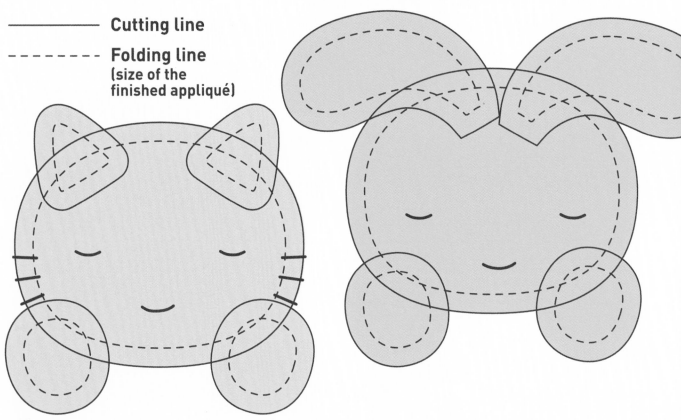

Patterns at 100% so no need to enlarge

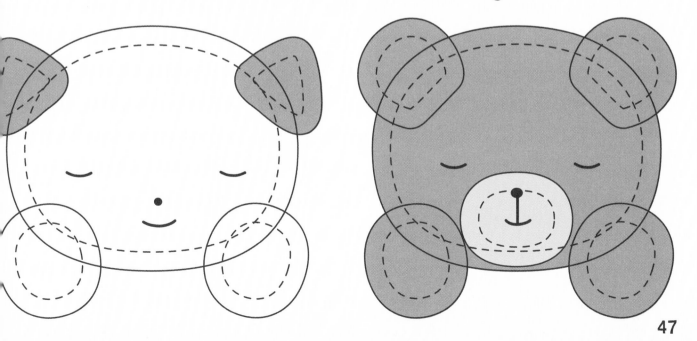

We're not Mary's lambs, we're lambs named Mary.
Spinning around and around on this mobile is very m
It's Mary Lambs Merry Mobile, baa.

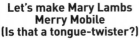

01
Let's make Mary Lambs Merry Mobile (Is that a tongue-twister?)

I'm Mary.

02
Cut the felt and fleece fabric according to the patterns

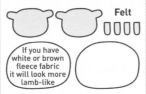

Felt

If you have white or brown fleece fabric it will look more lamb-like

Cut out the number of sheep you want spinning on your mobile

03
Prepare the string for the mobile

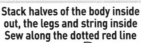

0.5-1 cm wide

60 cm long

Any type of string or ribbon is fine
Pick a color you like,
it can be thick or thin
If you want a long ribbon,
make it longer!

04
Embroider the eyes, nose and mouth

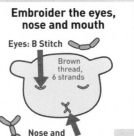

Eyes: B Stitch

Brown thread, 6 strands

Nose and mouth: B Stitch

05
Stack the halves and overlock stitch around

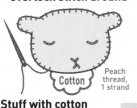

Cotton

Peach thread, 1 strand

Stuff with cotton and sew shut

06
Position the legs and string, sew them on to the front side of the body along the dotted blue line

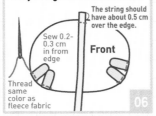

The string should have about 0.5 cm over the edge.

Sew 0.2-0.3 cm in from edge

Front

Thread same color as fleece fabric

07
Stack halves of the body inside out, the legs and string inside. Sew along the dotted red line

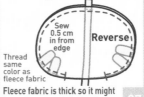

Sew 0.5 cm in from edge

Reverse

Thread same color as fleece fabric

Fleece fabric is thick so it might be easier to sew it by hand

08
Turn right side out and stuff with cotton then sew shut

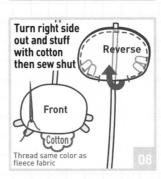

Reverse

Front

Cotton

Thread same color as fleece fabric

09
Position the head and sew it onto the body

Peach thread, 1 strand

Sew the back of the head to the body so the stitching won't show

10
Prepare wire

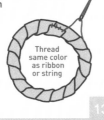

About 50 cm

There is no set thickness for the wire; however, very thick wire will be hard to bend into a circle and very thin wire might be too limp and lose its shape
If you already have a circular object you can use that instead

11
Twist the ends together to form a ring

If you want a bigger circle use a longer piece of wire

About 13 cm diameter

Owie! Wire is dangerous! Be careful!

12
Prepare a ribbon or string to cover the wire

1 cm wide

About 100 cm

Use any string or ribbon you want.
You can even use fabric. Pick any color.
It can be thick or thin.
(If it's thin, make it a little longer.)
Since the tips of the wire are sharp, it's best to wrap it.

13
Wrap the ribbon or string around the wire

Overlap the ribbon about 1/3-1/2 of the width
While wrapping, keep the ribbon pulled taut

When finished, sew the end

Thread same color as ribbon or string

14
Mark 4 places on the ring

Mark 4 spaces evenly

If you are using 6 sheep, make 6 evenly spaced marks

15
Tie a lamb's string onto the marked spot

About 10-20 cm long

16

You can have ribbons of different lengths, too

Tie on all four

17
Tie the ends of all the strings together making sure the mobile is balanced

18

You can attach the lambs to the baby's bed, or hang them on a wall or the ceiling. They're merry even without a mobile!

19

Even babies that don't sleep well will definitely fall asleep with these lambs! 1 lamb, 2 lambs...

Zzz Zzz Zzz

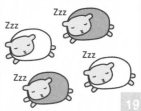
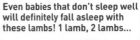

Mary Lambs Merry Mobile Materials

 Chalk pencils

 Scissors

 Sewing needle

 **Embroidery needle**
Use for the eyes, nose and mouth

Ruler

Fleece fabric

White or Brown like a lamb

Stretch thread
Same color as fabric

Felt

Peach

Embroidery thread

Peach

Brown

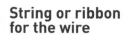

Cotton

Ribbon or String for the mobile

0.5-1 cm wide

60 cm long

String or ribbon for the wire

1 cm wide

100 cm long

Regular thread
Same color as ribbon or string

Wire

50 cm

About the Ribbon or String

It can be either ribbon or string, in any color.
Thicker or thinner is also ok.
(If you use a thin ribbon make it a little longer so there will be enough to cover the wire.)
You can use the same ribbon or string for the ring and for the lambs.
You can also cut fabric and use it to wrap the wire as well.

About the Wire

The thickness is up to you, but if it is very thick it will be hard to twist into a ring.
If it is very thin, it will be too limp and lose its shape.
If you have something circular, you can use that instead of wire, too.

Zzz  Zzz  Zzz  Zzz

Mary Lambs Merry Mobile Patterns

Patterns at 100% so no need to enlarge

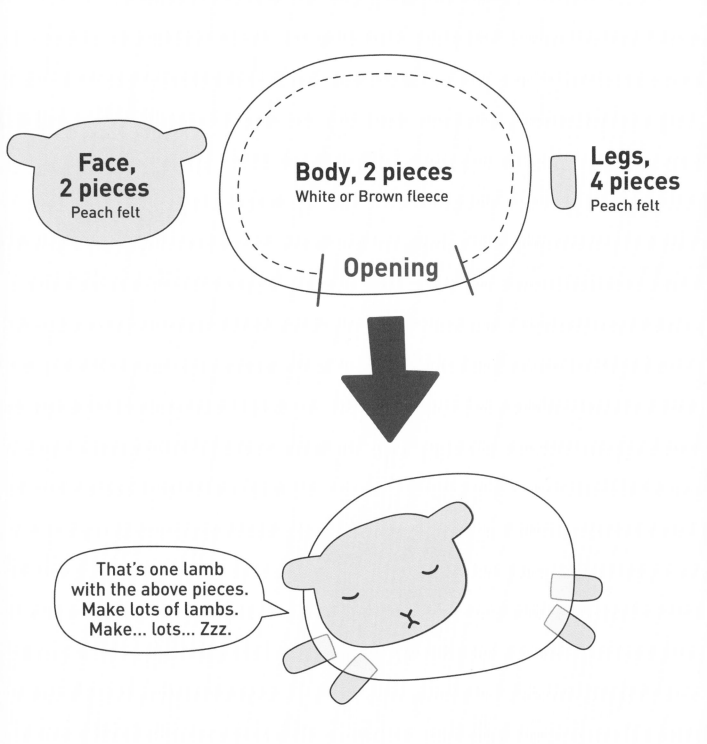

Face, 2 pieces
Peach felt

Body, 2 pieces
White or Brown fleece

Opening

Legs, 4 pieces
Peach felt

That's one lamb with the above pieces. Make lots of lambs. Make... lots... Zzz.

Baby can't yet say,
"It would be so cute to have
embroidery on all my stuff!"
But it would be really cute, so
let's embroider a bunch of things.

How to Do Easy Embroidery

01 — Adding embroidery to your baby's stuff will make it all very cute!

Bib · Mitten · Socks · Hanky

02 — It's easy! Anyone can do it. Let's embroider!

03 — This is the basic B Stitch. This is a diagram of what a B Stitch looks like.

1 Out
3 Out   2 In

B Stitch

04 — Copy the pattern on a piece of tracing paper

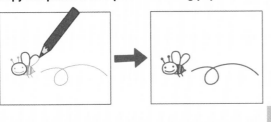

05 — Position your embroidery

Layer in order from bottom to top

- Fabric to embroider
- Chalk paper (The pattern will transfer onto fabric as you trace over the chalk paper.)
- Tracing paper with pattern

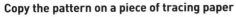

06 — Trace pattern onto fabric

You don't need to press too hard for it to transfer
It may come out too thick or the paper might rip if you press too hard

07 — B Stitch along traced lines. (Embroidery thread, 3 strands)

Thread in any color

Sew stitches as close together as possible
Don't pull too hard or the fabric will wrinkle!

08 — There's no particular order for stitching. Stitch however you want. For sections that are near each other, carry over the thread under the surface to the next section and keep sewing with the same thread.

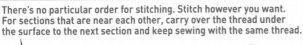

09 —
Antennae: FN Stitch, turn 3 times (3 strands)
Eyes: FN Stitch, turn 3 times (3 strands)
Tail: S-Stitch (3 strands)
Stripes: Satin stitch (3 strands)

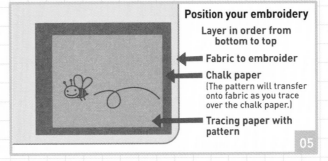

10 — Bumble, bumble!

Done!

11 — Here's a summary of the instructions for Easy Embroidery.

B Stitch for long lines and curves

S-Stitch for short lines
Satin stitch to fill in color

- FN Stitch, turn once, for small circles.
- FN Stitch, turn twice, for medium.
- FN Stitch, turn 3 times, for large circles.

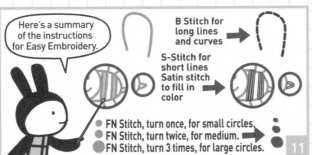

12 — The appliqués on page 20 are also easy to embroider They're cute, too!

Try embroidering patterns and pictures other than the ones in the book!

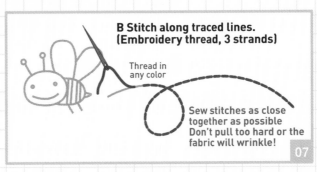

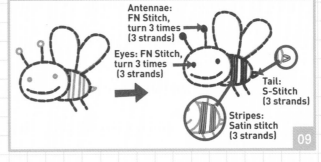

Easy Embroidery Materials

Chalk pencils

Scissors

Embroidery needle

Embroidery thread
Any color

Fabric things to embroider

A plain handkerchief, bib or anything you want to embroider

Tracing paper
for patterns

Chalk paper
Used when transferring the pattern onto the fabric

Easy Embroidery Designs

Designs are at 100%, but you can enlarge or reduce as you wish

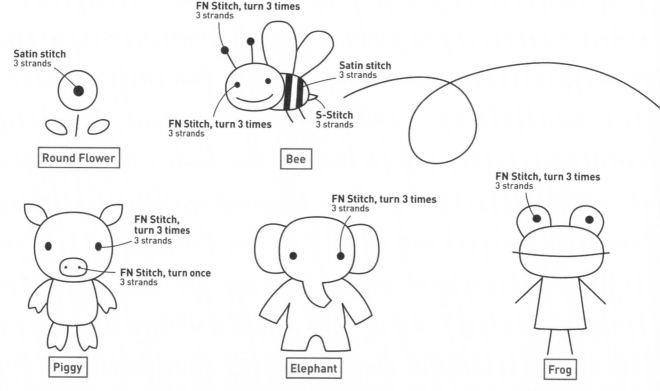

Satin stitch
3 strands

Round Flower

FN Stitch, turn 3 times
3 strands

Satin stitch
3 strands

FN Stitch, turn 3 times
3 strands

S-Stitch
3 strands

Bee

FN Stitch, turn 3 times
3 strands

FN Stitch, turn 3 times
3 strands

FN Stitch, turn 3 times
3 strands

FN Stitch, turn once
3 strands

Piggy

Elephant

Frog

If no stitch instructions are given, use a B Stitch (3 strands)

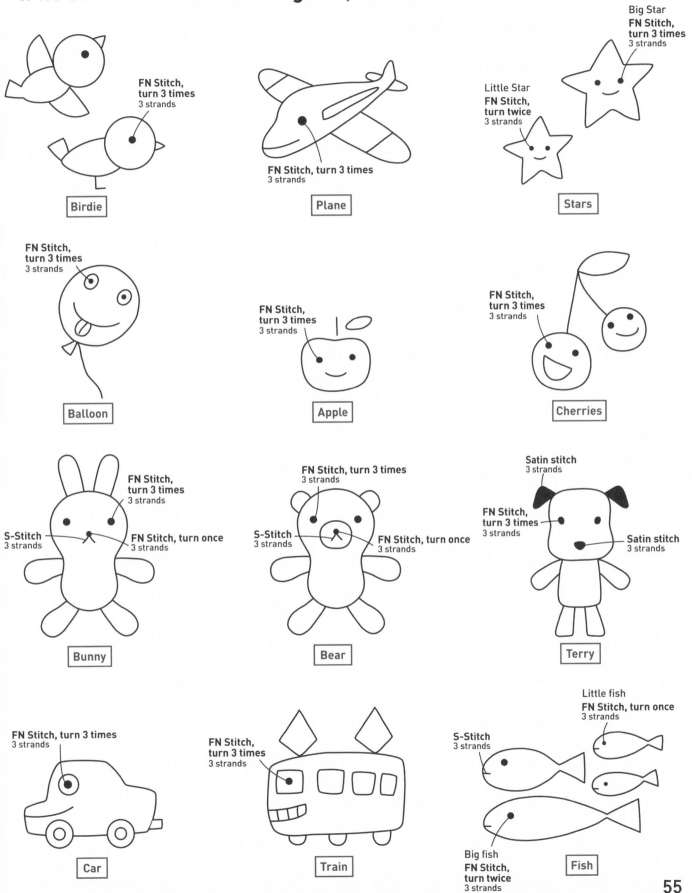

Birdie

FN Stitch, turn 3 times
3 strands

Plane

FN Stitch, turn 3 times
3 strands

Stars

Big Star
FN Stitch, turn 3 times
3 strands

Little Star
FN Stitch, turn twice
3 strands

Balloon

FN Stitch, turn 3 times
3 strands

Apple

FN Stitch, turn 3 times
3 strands

Cherries

FN Stitch, turn 3 times
3 strands

Bunny

FN Stitch, turn 3 times
3 strands

S-Stitch
3 strands

FN Stitch, turn once
3 strands

Bear

FN Stitch, turn 3 times
3 strands

S-Stitch
3 strands

FN Stitch, turn once
3 strands

Terry

Satin stitch
3 strands

FN Stitch, turn 3 times
3 strands

Satin stitch
3 strands

Car

FN Stitch, turn 3 times
3 strands

Train

FN Stitch, turn 3 times
3 strands

Fish

Little fish
FN Stitch, turn once
3 strands

S-Stitch
3 strands

Big fish
FN Stitch, turn twice
3 strands

55

A bib is a fabulous fashion item for baby.
Put a stylish bandana bib on your baby to make him stand out in the crowd!

How to Make a Bandana Bib

01
Food spills on his clothes

02
Drool makes his clothes all wet

03
He's still a baby but... he doesn't like to wear a bib

Baby Bad Guy

04
He might hate wearing bibs, because they make him look, well, like a baby

05
Let's make a bandana bib for the willful little one. Then it'll be a bandana, not just a bib.

06
Let's embroider a bandana-like pattern on it. Make it stylish!

07
Cut the fabric according to the patterns in any color

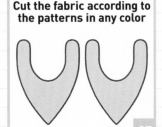

08
Prepare the Velcro

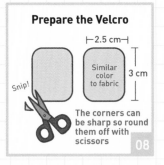

├─2.5 cm─┤

Similar color to fabric

3 cm

Snip!

The corners can be sharp so round them off with scissors

09
Trace pattern onto a piece of tracing paper

If you use the patterns on pages 54 and 55 for Easy Embroidery you can make a cute design

Trace a few onto the paper in different spots and you'll have your design

10
Choose where you want to position your embroidery and transfer with chalk paper

Layer in this order from bottom to top

→ **Fabric to embroider**

→ **Chalk paper** (The pattern will transfer onto fabric as you trace over the chalk paper)

→ **Tracing paper with pattern**

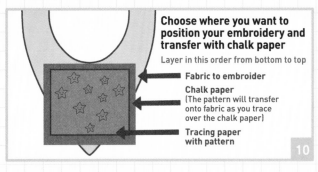

11
Trace pattern gently onto fabric

Stitch along traced lines
Please refer to page 53 for embroidery instructions

12
Stack the halves of bib inside out and sew along the dotted red line

Reverse

Cut along the blue lines

Reverse

Make incisions so the curve comes out neat and smooth
Be careful not to cut the thread!

Turn right side out

Reverse

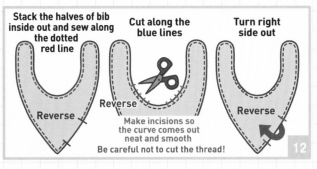

13
Put your hand inside and shape the bib

Smooth out and then iron
It will come out neater if you iron along the fold

Sew the opening shut

Thread same color as fabric

Front

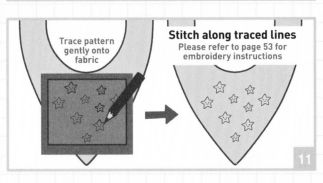

14
Sew around the edges of the Velcro

Be sure to align the Velcro before attaching

Front   Back

Done!

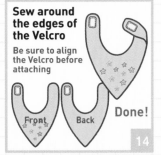

15
I feel like a grown-up! Yay!

Bandana Bib Materials

Chalk pencils

Scissors

Sewing machine

Sewing needle
Used to sew the bib

Embroidery needle
Used for embroidery

Iron

Tracing paper
To trace patterns

Chalk paper for fabric
Used to transfer patterns onto fabric

Ruler

Bandana Bib cotton fabric

Any color

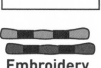

Regular thread
Same color as fabric

Embroidery thread
Any color

Velcro
2.5 cm x 2.5 cm, 1 piece in any color

Bandana Bib Designs

Enlarge to 200% for ideal size

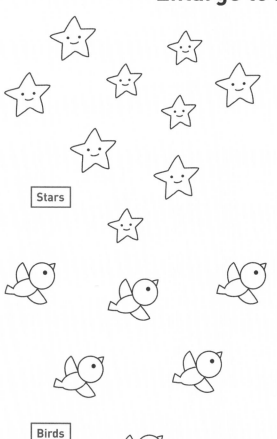

Stars

Apples

Birds

Fish

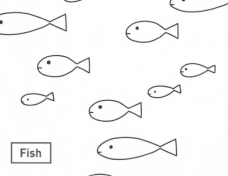

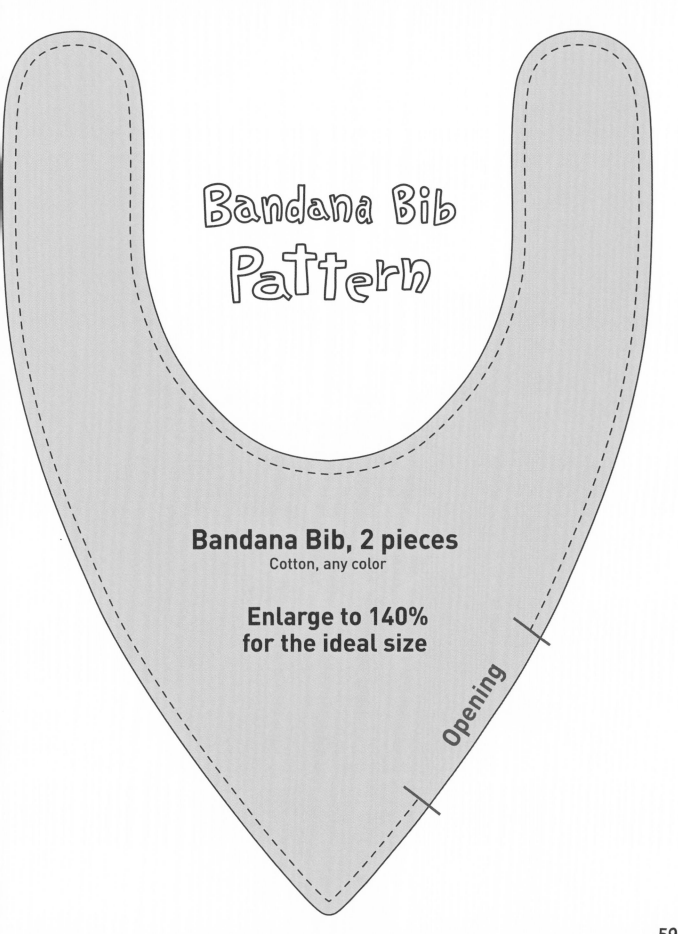

Bandana Bib Pattern

Bandana Bib, 2 pieces
Cotton, any color

**Enlarge to 140%
for the ideal size**

Opening

Do you know what's inside these pouches?
Try and guess from the appliqués on the front.
Can you guess?
The answers are on the next page!

How to Make Handy Pouches

01

Babies need lots of things, so going out can be tough. It's convenient to have things in separate pouches, so make a lot! You can put appliqués on them so you know what's inside!

A change of clothes
Food
Shoes
Toys
Diapers

02

First decide the length and width of the pouch

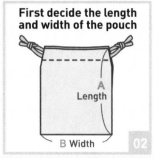

A Length
B Width

03

Make a pattern

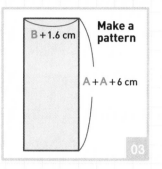

B + 1.6 cm
A + A + 6 cm

04

Transfer pattern onto fabric and cut out

Sew edges of the fabric with a zig-zag or overlock machine (to prevent the fabric from fraying)

05

Fold in half inside out
Sew along the dotted red line, leaving 7 cm open at the top

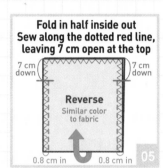

7 cm down
7 cm down
Reverse
Similar color to fabric
0.8 cm in
0.8 cm in

06

Fold both edges of the top in the direction of the red arrows

About 1 cm

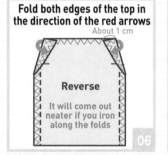

Reverse
It will come out neater if you iron along the folds

07

Fold top down 3 cm

3 cm
Reverse
It will come out neater if you iron along the fold

08

Sew along the dotted red line 2.5 cm down from the top

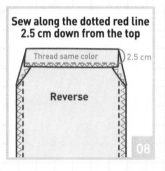

Thread same color
2.5 cm
Reverse

09

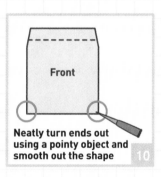

Turn right side out
Reverse
Front

10

Front
Neatly turn ends out using a pointy object and smooth out the shape

11

When you finish making the pouch, insert a drawstring. You can use a cord or make a drawstring from the same fabric as the purse.

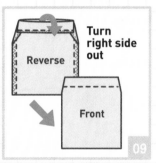

12

It will come out neater if you iron the fold

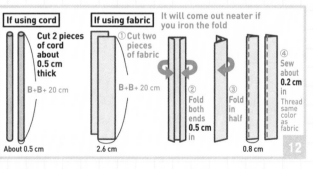

If using cord | Cut 2 pieces of cord about 0.5 cm thick
B+B+ 20 cm
About 0.5 cm

If using fabric | ① Cut two pieces of fabric
B+B+ 20 cm
2.6 cm
② Fold both ends 0.5 cm in
③ Fold in half
0.8 cm
④ Sew about 0.2 cm in Thread same color as fabric

13

Thread drawstring with a bodkin then tie string

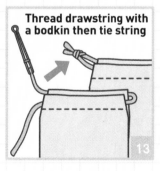

14

Thread drawstring through other side then tie

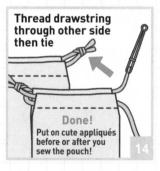

Done!
Put on cute appliqués before or after you sew the pouch!

15

Size of bags on opposite page

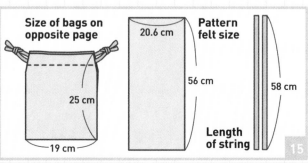

25 cm
19 cm

Pattern felt size
20.6 cm
56 cm
58 cm
Length of string

16

How to add appliqués

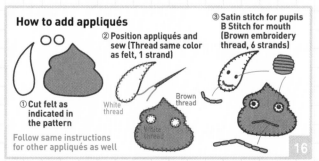

① Cut felt as indicated in the pattern

② Position appliqués and sew (Thread same color as felt, 1 strand)
White thread

③ Satin stitch for pupils B Stitch for mouth (Brown embroidery thread, 6 strands)
Brown thread
White thread

Follow same instructions for other appliqués as well

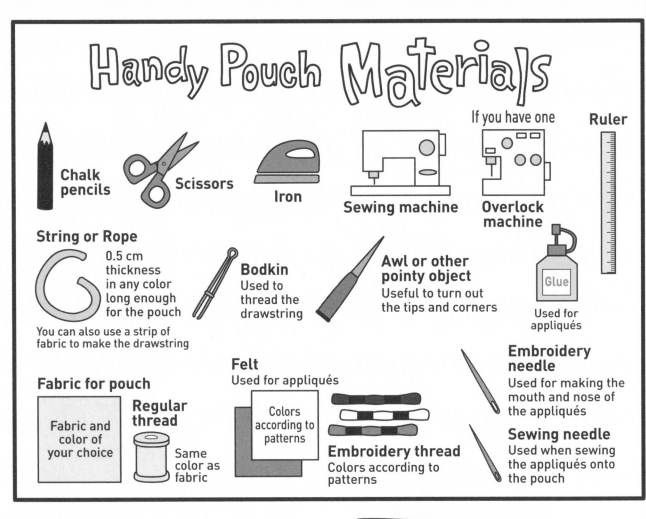

Handy Pouch Materials

Chalk pencils

Scissors

Iron

Sewing machine

Overlock machine
If you have one

Ruler

String or Rope
0.5 cm thickness in any color long enough for the pouch
You can also use a strip of fabric to make the drawstring

Bodkin
Used to thread the drawstring

Awl or other pointy object
Useful to turn out the tips and corners

Glue
Used for appliqués

Fabric for pouch
Fabric and color of your choice

Regular thread
Same color as fabric

Felt
Used for appliqués
Colors according to patterns

Embroidery thread
Colors according to patterns

Embroidery needle
Used for making the mouth and nose of the appliqués

Sewing needle
Used when sewing the appliqués onto the pouch

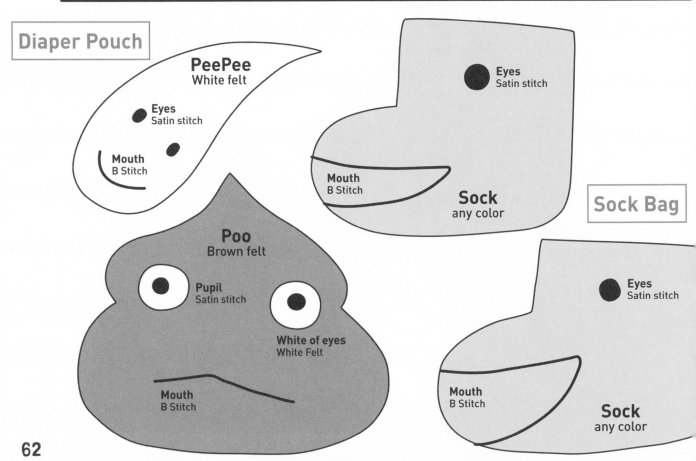

Diaper Pouch

PeePee
White felt

Eyes
Satin stitch

Mouth
B Stitch

Poo
Brown felt

Pupil
Satin stitch

White of eyes
White Felt

Mouth
B Stitch

Eyes
Satin stitch

Mouth
B Stitch

Sock
any color

Sock Bag

Eyes
Satin stitch

Mouth
B Stitch

Sock
any color

Handy Pouch Appliqué Patterns

Patterns at 100% so no need to enlarge

uth and Eyes:
in stitch, brown thread, 6 strands
B Stitch, brown thread, 6 strands

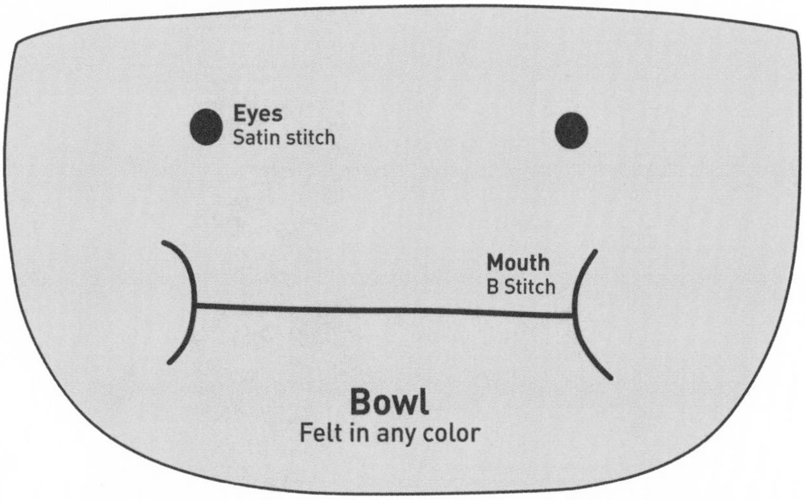

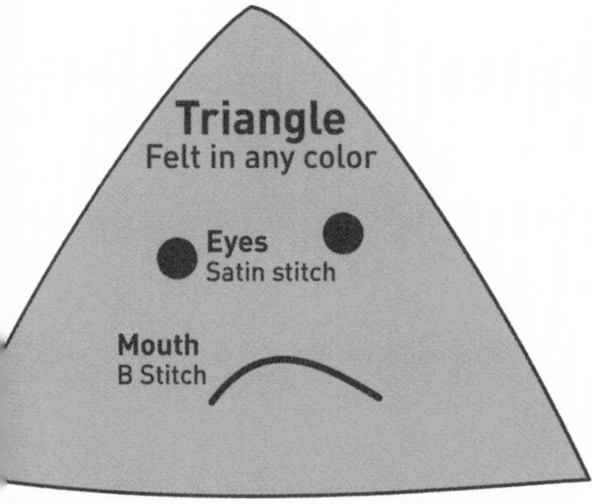

Triangle
Felt in any color

Eyes
Satin stitch

Mouth
B Stitch

Eyes
Satin stitch

Mouth
B Stitch

Bowl
Felt in any color

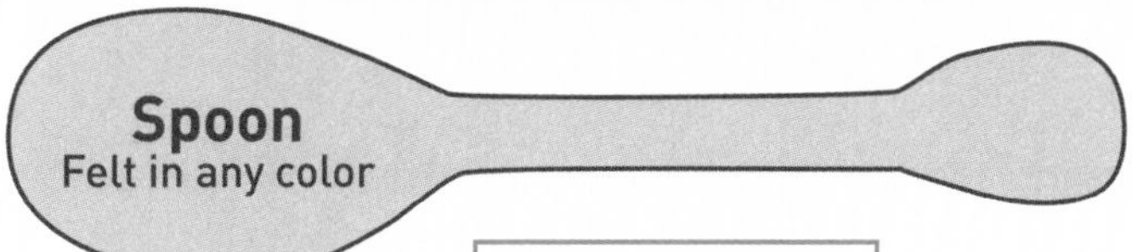

Spoon
Felt in any color

Food Pouch

Eyes
Satin stitch

Mouth
B Stitch

Square
Felt in any color

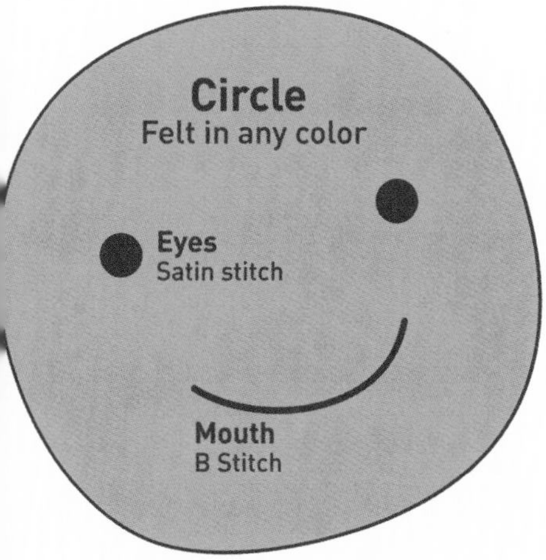

Pupil
Satin stitch

White of eyes
White Felt

Mouth
White Felt

Circle
Felt in any color

Eyes
Satin stitch

Mouth
B Stitch

T-shirt
Felt in any color

Legs
B Stitch,
brown thread,
6 strands

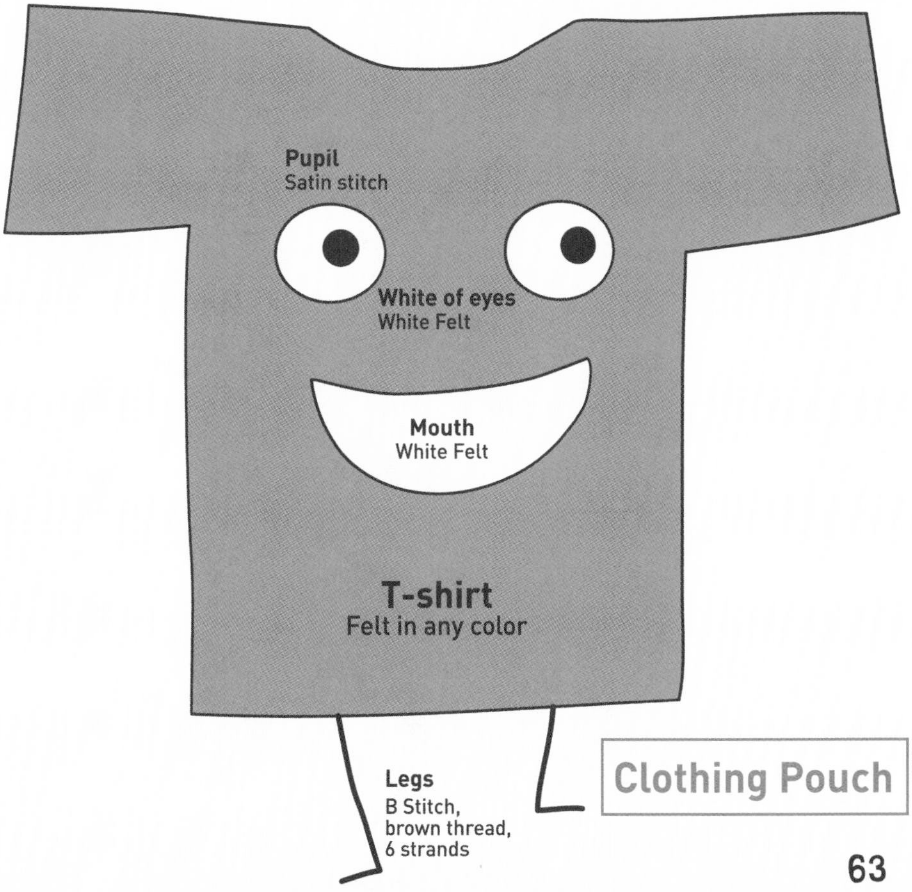

Clothing Pouch

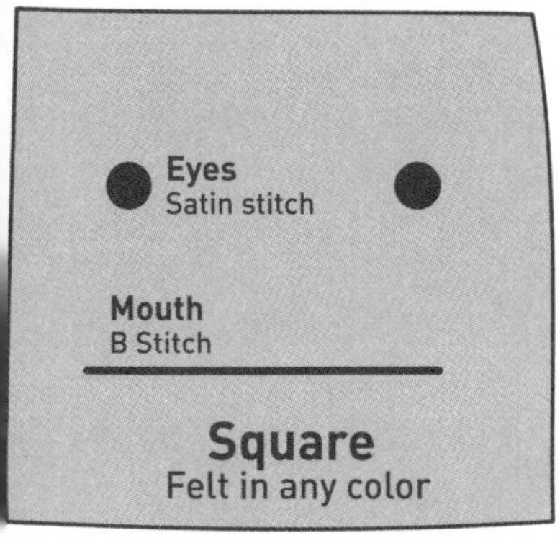

Toy Pouch

63

"Tell me how tall I am!"
"Wait, your ears don't count, right?"
"Yeah they do!"

01
Pick any fabric you want and cut two pieces the same size

The fabric can be any color you like, but keep in mind that Tongue's appliqué is white so a dark color is best

27 cm
102 cm

Tongue is a white dog →

02
Stack halves inside out and sew along the dotted white line

Sew 1 cm in
Do not sew the opening

1 cm in

Opening is 15-20 cm

Reverse
Thread same color as fabric
Opening

If you want to add hooks for hanging
Insert strings as shown before sewing

Reverse | Front

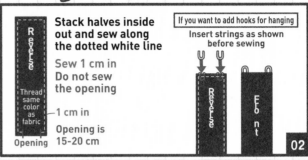

03
Turn right side out and sew opening shut

Front

Thread same color as fabric

04
Neatly turn corners out using an awl or other pointy object

It'll be easier to sew if you iron first

Front

05
After sewing it will be this size

25 cm
100 cm

If it's a little off it's ok

5 cm (×19 listed)
95 cm, 90 cm, 85 cm, 80 cm, 75 cm, 70 cm, 65 cm, 60 cm, 55 cm, 50 cm, 45 cm, 40 cm, 35 cm, 30 cm, 25 cm, 20 cm, 15 cm, 10 cm, 5 cm

Measure with a ruler and draw lines with a chalk pencil

Measure from 5 cm to 95 cm, 5 cm apart

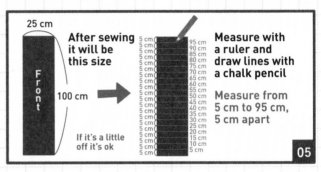

06
Sew along the lines (white embroidery thread, 6 strands)

White thread, 6 strands

Stitch however you like – a small stitch or a wide stitch

Any stitch is fine

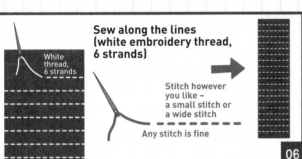

07
Cut felt according to the pattern for Tongue (6 dogs)

Face
Body
Eyes ::::: Nose • • • • • Mouth ▾▾▾▾▾▾
Tongue's numbers 1 2 3 4 5 6

Apply the nose and eyes to each
Use any color for Tongue's numbers, but a dark color, the same as the chart, is recommended

Again, Tongue is a white dog

10 20 30 40 50 60 70 80 90

Cut the numbers from felt according to the pattern

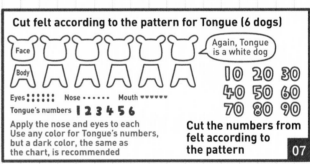

08
Position Tongue's eyes, nose, and tongue Glue lightly then cross-stitch

Thread same color as felt
Red thread

09
B Stitch the nose line and the mouth

Thread same color as nose, 6 strands
Red thread, 6 strands

10
Position Tongue's numbers, glue lightly then cross-stitch

2

Thread same color as numbers

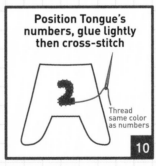

11
About 0.5 cm
Glue

Apply glue to the top of the body and attach the face

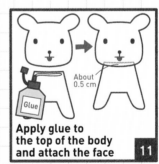

12
Choose a position for all the Tongues Glue lightly, then cross-stitch

White thread

13
Choose a position for the chart's numbers, glue lightly, then cross-stitch

White thread

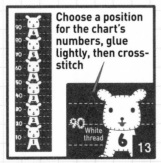

14
If you make Tongue's Height Measure, you can hang it on the wall and measure baby's height every day! Babies that can't stand yet can be measured lying on the floor.

Done!

Tongue's Height Measure Materials

Chalk pencils

Scissors

Glue

Iron

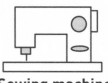
Sewing machine

Ruler

Embroidery needle
Used for running stitches, B Stitches, etc.

Sewing needle
Used for sewing on the appliqués and cross-stitching

String
Used to create hanging loops

Awl or other pointy object
Handy for turning the corners right side out

Felt for Tongue

| White | Dark color (eyes and nose) | Red | Any color (for numbers) |

Fabric
27 cm by 102 cm, 2 pieces

Any color (dark is best)

Regular thread

Same color as fabric

Embroidery thread

White

Red

Dark color (to match eyes and nose)

Color (to match numbers)

Numbers for chart, 1 of each
White felt

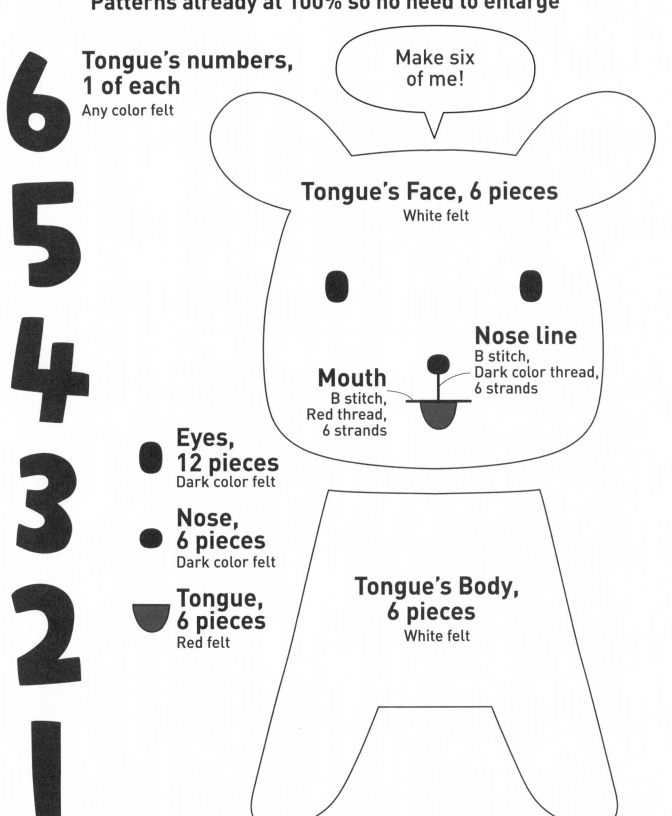

Appliqué Patterns

Patterns already at 100% so no need to enlarge

**Tongue's numbers,
1 of each**
Any color felt

Make six
of me!

Tongue's Face, 6 pieces
White felt

Nose line
B stitch,
Dark color thread,
6 strands

Mouth
B stitch,
Red thread,
6 strands

**Eyes,
12 pieces**
Dark color felt

**Nose,
6 pieces**
Dark color felt

**Tongue,
6 pieces**
Red felt

**Tongue's Body,
6 pieces**
White felt

Every baby has a cute name.
Moms and dads think really hard to give
their baby a good name.
We're sure babies love their names, too.

How to Make Cute Names

Her name is White Rabbit

01

His name is Bear

02

A Cute Name appliqué is a way to make a cute appliqué for a cute name.

03

Let's try making cute appliqués for their names.

04

Cut felt according to the patterns for the letters

Rabbit
BEAR

Any color felt

05

Cut felt according to patterns for flowers and stars

Flowers for White Rabbit, stars for Bear, or the other way around

06

Stitch the middle of the flower

FN Stitch, turn twice
White thread, 6 strands

07

Cut the patterns for White Rabbit and Bear

08

Make White Rabbit's face

Eyes: FN Stitch, turn twice

Brown thread, 2 strands

Nose: FN Stitch, turn once

Mouth: S-Stitch

09

Make Bear's face

Eyes: FN Stitch, turn twice

Glue on white of eyes and muzzle

Nose: FN Stitch, turn once

Brown thread, 2 strands

Mouth: S-Stitch

10

Apply glue to the edges of the clothing and ears and glue face on top

11

Line up the letters

Rabbit

12

Arrange the White Rabbit (or Bear) and the flower (or star) appliqués

For this look, tuck the clothes under the letter

Position and glue lightly

13

Cross-stitch edges of felt

Done!

Thread same color as felt

14

When you do the cute name appliqué, use your imagination to make it even cuter!

15

Let's put cute names on lots of things!

16

White Rabbit and Bear are really happy with their name appliqués!

17

Cute Names Materials

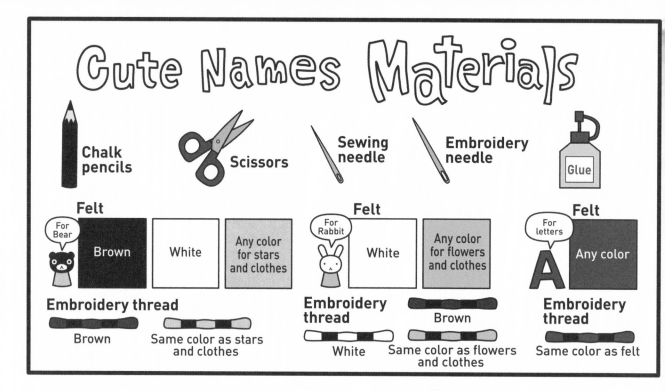

Chalk pencils

Scissors

Sewing needle

Embroidery needle

Glue

Felt

For Bear

Brown | White | Any color for stars and clothes

Embroidery thread

Brown | Same color as stars and clothes

Felt

For Rabbit

White | Any color for flowers and clothes

Embroidery thread

White | Brown | Same color as flowers and clothes

Felt

For letters

A | Any color

Embroidery thread

Same color as felt

Cute Names Patterns

Ears, 2 pieces
Brown felt

Face, 1 piece
Brown felt

White of eyes, 2 pieces
White felt

Muzzle, 1 piece
White felt

Clothes, 1 piece
Any color felt

Ears, 2 pieces
White felt

Face, 1 piece
White felt

Clothes, 1 piece
Any color felt

Enlarge for bigger patterns, shrink for smaller ones
Make them at any size you wa
(The name appliqués shown on pages 68 and 72 were made at 10

Eyes: FN Stitch, turn twice

Nose: FN Stitch, turn once

Mouth: S-Stitch

Brown thread, 2 strands

Bear

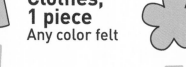

Eyes: FN Stitch, turn twice

Nose: FN Stitch, turn once

Mouth: S-Stitch

Brown thread, 2 strands

Rabbit

Flower, 1 piece
Any color felt

Middle: FN Stitch, turn twice

White thread, 6 strands

Flower

Star, 1 pie
Any co

Star

71

Let's put appliqués of baby's name
on all of the baby's things.
It would be cute to put appliqués of mommy's
name on all of mommy's stuff, too!

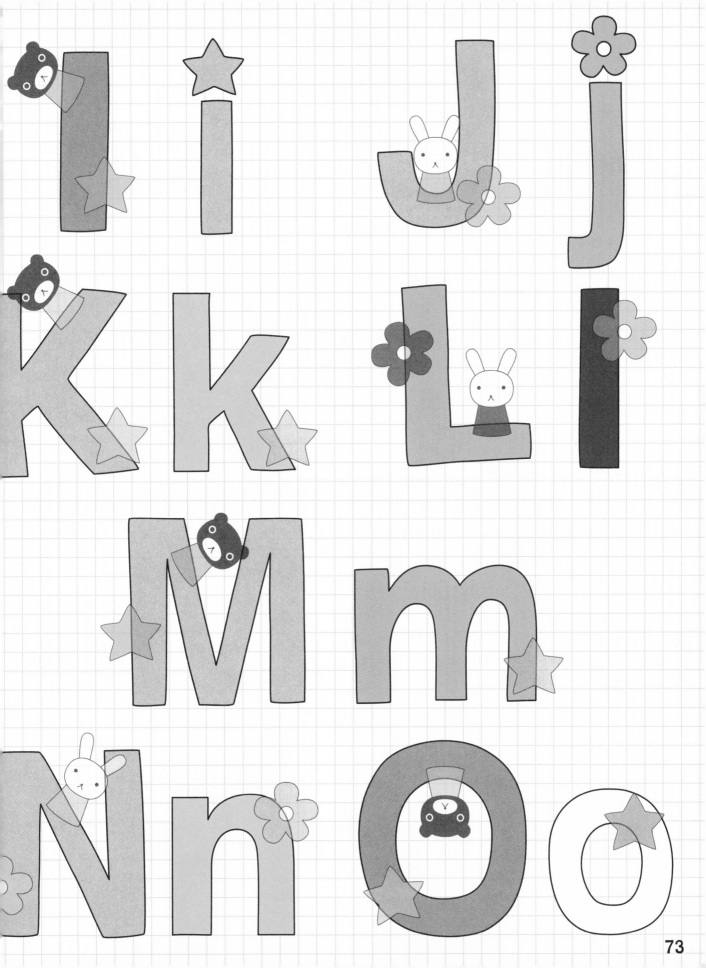

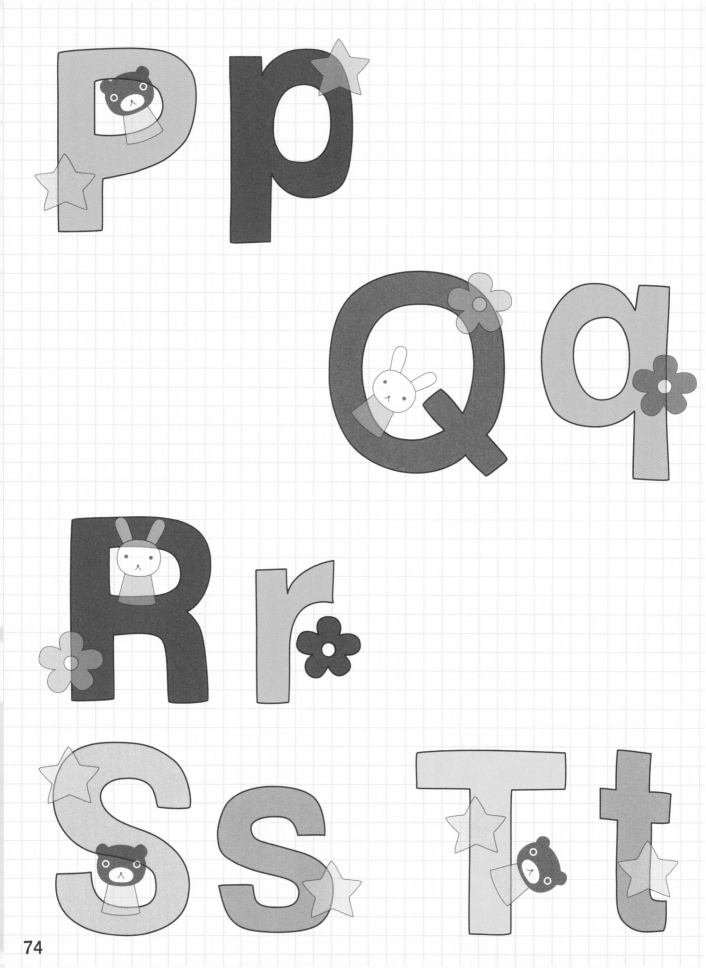

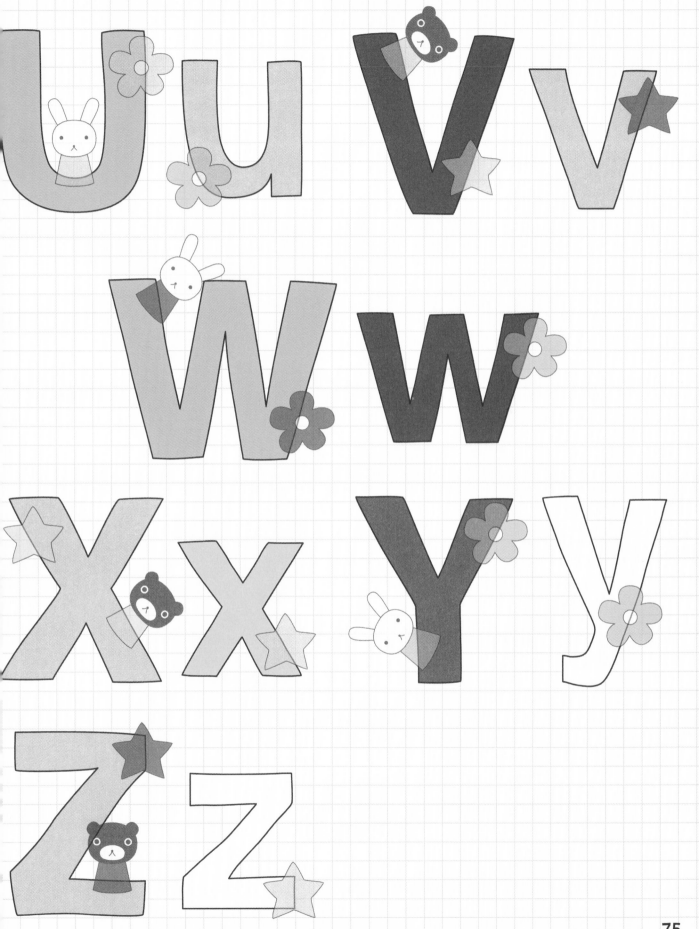

This cake sure looks yummy, but you can't really eat it.
Happy Birthday! May you quickly grow big and strong!

How to Make Cake Boy

01
Cut felt according to cake patterns

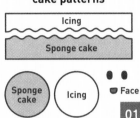

- Icing
- Sponge cake
- Sponge cake
- Icing
- Face

02
Cut felt according to strawberry and candle patterns

Strawberries 4 pieces

Candle

03
Prepare 5 pairs of Velcro according to pattern

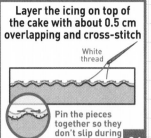

White

04
Layer the icing on top of the cake with about 0.5 cm overlapping and cross-stitch

White thread

Pin the pieces together so they don't slip during sewing

05
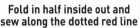

Brown thread

Freckles: FN stitch, turn once

Red thread

Mouth: B stitch
Red thread, 6 strands

1 Out
3 Out
2 In

Position the face, glue the tongue and eyes lightly then cross-stitch

06
Fold in half inside out and sew along the dotted red line

1 cm in

Reverse

07
Sew the Velcro onto the icing top

White thread

Attach the fuzzy side of the Velcro

08
① **Stack the top and sides of the cake inside out**

Top
Velcro should be inside

Reverse

② **First do a simple running stitch to sew the top and sides together 1 cm from the edge**

White thread

Reverse

③ **After the running stitch, machine sew or do a close hand stitch**

White thread

Reverse

09
① **Turn over and align the bottom and sides of the cake inside out**

Bottom

Reverse

② **Sew together 1 cm inside the edge of the base First do a simple running stitch Do not sew the opening**

Light brown thread
Reverse
Opening

Reverse

③ **After the running stitch, machine sew or do a close hand stitch Do not sew the opening**

Light brown thread
Reverse

Reverse

10
Turn right side out and stuff with cotton

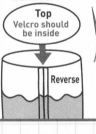

Cotton

11
Sew shut

Light brown thread

12
① **Stack strawberry halves inside out and sew along the dotted white line**

Red thread
Red thread

② **Turn right side out**

Cotton

③ **Sew along the dotted blue line**

Red thread

Front

④ **Stuff with cotton, sew edges and pull thread tight to close**

Tight!

Red thread

⑤ **Place the leaves on top and cross-stitch along the yellow lines**

Green thread

⑥ **Cross-stitch the Velcro on Sew on the scratchy side this time**

White thread

13
① **Fold the candle in half inside out Sew along the dotted blue line**

Yellow thread

White thread ② **Cross-stitch the inner flame onto the outer flame**

③ **Stack the two halves and overlock stitch around**

Red thread

④ **Insert the flame into the candle and sew along the dotted blue line**

⑤ **Turn right side out and stuff with cotton**

Yellow thread

⑥ **Cross-stitch the Velcro onto the candle base**

White thread

⑦ **Overlock stitch the bottom and sides of candle**

Yellow thread
Sew scratchy side of Velcro

14

We made 1 cake, 1 candle and 4 strawberries!

15
You can unattach the strawberries and the candle and play with them!

Make me look yummy!

Done!

77

Cake Boy Materials

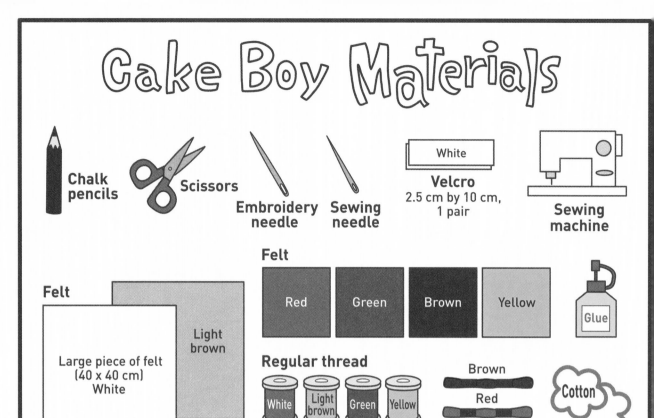

- Chalk pencils
- Scissors
- Embroidery needle
- Sewing needle
- Velcro — White — 2.5 cm by 10 cm, 1 pair
- Sewing machine

Felt
- Large piece of felt (40 x 40 cm) White
- Light brown

Felt
- Red
- Green
- Brown
- Yellow
- Glue

Regular thread
- White
- Light brown
- Green
- Yellow

You can use embroidery thread for white, green and yellow

Embroidery thread
- Brown
- Red

Cotton

Cake Boy Patterns

Cake Boy's face, strawberries and candles at 100% so no need to enlarge

Strawberry leav[es]
4 pieces
Green felt

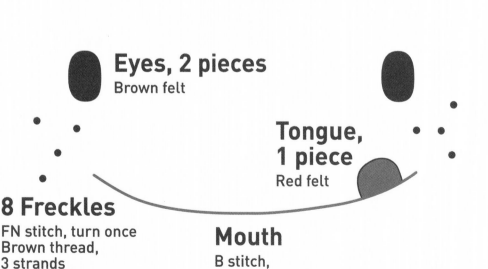

Eyes, 2 pieces
Brown felt

Tongue, 1 piece
Red felt

8 Freckles
FN stitch, turn once
Brown thread,
3 strands

Mouth
B stitch,
Red thread, 6 strands

Strawberries,
8 pieces
Red felt

Sides and base of Cake:
Enlarge to 200% for the ideal size

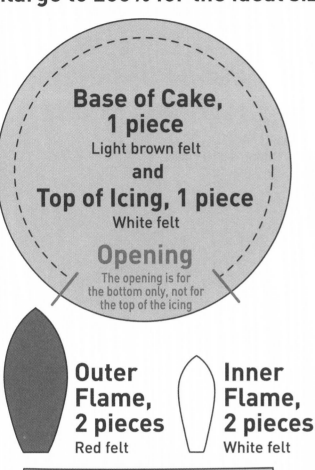

**Base of Cake,
1 piece**
Light brown felt
and
Top of Icing, 1 piece
White felt

Opening
The opening is for the bottom only, not for the top of the icing

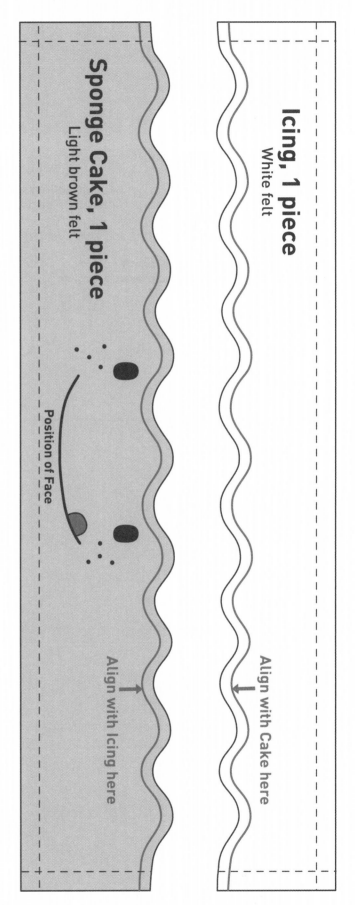

Sponge Cake, 1 piece
Light brown felt

Position of Face

Align with Icing here

Icing, 1 piece
White felt

Align with Cake here

**Outer
Flame,
2 pieces**
Red felt

**Inner
Flame,
2 pieces**
White felt

**Side of Candle,
1 piece**
Yellow felt

**Bottom of Candle,
1 piece**
Yellow felt

**Velcro,
5 pairs**
White (for the candles and strawberries)

ARANZI ARONZO

Aranzi Aronzo is a company that
"makes what it feels like the way it feels like and then sells the stuff."
Established in 1991 in Osaka. Kinuyo Saito and Yoko Yomura team.
Other than original miscellany, Aranzi Aronzo also makes picture books and exhibits.
Other books include *The Cute Book, The Bad Book, Aranzi Machine Gun vols. 1-3,
Cute Dolls, Fun Dolls, Cute Stuff,* and *The Complete Aranzi Hour.*

http://www.aranziaronzo.com
http://www.vertical-inc.com/aranzi_aronzo

Translation — Jessica Hatakeda

Copyright © 2009 by Aranzi Aronzo

All rights reserved.

Published by Vertical, Inc., New York.

Originally published in Japanese as *Konnichiwa Akachan*
by Bunka Shuppankyoku, Tokyo, 2008.

ISBN 978-1-934287-45-3

Manufactured in The United States of America

First American Edition

Vertical, Inc.
www.vertical-inc.com